The National Theatre
The Abbey and Peacock Theatres

On Such as We

By Billy Roche

D1333764

The National Theatre gratefully acknowledges the financial
support from the Arts Council/An Chomhairle Ealaíon

On Such as We

By Billy Roche

The play is set in Wexford

There will be one interval of 15 minutes

Cast in order of appearance

Oweney	Brendan Gleeson
Leonard	Laurence Kinlan
Matt	Jason Gilroy
Richie	Frank McDonald
Eddie	David Herlihy
Maeve	Antoine Byrne
Sally	Pauline Hutton
Director	Wilson Milam
Set Designer	Bláithín Sheerin
Costume Designer	Catherine Fay
Lighting Designer	Tina MacHugh
Sound	Dave Nolan
Stage Director	Audrey Hession
Assistant Stage Manager	Stephen Dempsey
Voice Coach	Andrea Ainsworth
Set	Abbey Theatre Workshop
Costumes	Abbey Theatre Wardrobe Department

Please note that the text of the play which appears in this volume may be changed during the rehearsal process and appear in a slightly altered form in performance.

Billy Roche *Author*

Billy began his career as a singer/musician, forming The Roche Band in the late seventies. His first novel, **Tumbling Down,** was published by Wolfhound Press in 1986. His first stage play **A Handful of Stars** was staged at the Bush Theatre in 1988. This was followed by **Poor Beast in the Rain. Belfry** completed this powerful trilogy at the Bush Theatre. All three plays became know as **The Wexford Trilogy** and were performed in their entirety at the Bush, the Peacock and the Theatre Royal, Wexford. His fourth play **Amphibians** was commissioned by the RSC and performed at the Barbican. This was followed by **The Cavalcaders** at the Peacock Theatre and the Royal Court, London. He wrote the screenplay for **Trojan Eddie** which was directed by Gillies Mackinnon and starred Stephen Rea and Richard Harris. Billy has been Writer-in-Residence at the Bush, Writer-in-Association with Druid and the Abbey Theatre. As an actor Billy has appeared in **A Handful of Stars,** Bush Theatre, **Aristocrats,** Hampstead Theatre, **Poor Beast in the Rain** and **The Cavalcaders.**

Wilson Milam *Director*

Wilson's credits in Ireland and UK include **A Life of the Mind,** Donmar Warehouse, **Lieutenant of Inishmore,** RSC, **The Wexford Trilogy,** Tricycle Theatre, Lowry Theatre, Gateway Theatre, **Hurlyburly** (Olivier Award, Best Play 1997), The Peter Hall Company, Old Vic Theatre, Queen's Theatre, London, **Bug,** Gate Theatre, London and **Killer Joe** (Scotsman Fringe First Award), Vaudeville Theatre, Bush Theatre, London, Traverse Theatre, Edinburgh Festival. He directed staged readings of **Hurrah at Last,** Rough Magic Theatre, Dublin and **Tom and Jerry,** Gate Theatre, London. His work in the United States includes **Closer,** Berkeley Repertory Theatre, San Francisco, **Bug,** Wooly Mammoth Theatre, Washington DC, **Killer Joe,** Soho Playhouse, 29th St Repertory Theatre, New York, Next Theatre, Chicago, **Pot Mom,** Steppenwolf Theatre Company, Chicago, **The Caine Mutiny, Court Martial,** A Red Orchid Theatre, Chicago, **Skeleton,** Shattered Globe Theatre, Chicago, **Witness to Temptation,** American Blues Theatre, Chicago. He directed staged readings of **Breath Short of Breathing,** New York Stage and film, **Poughkeepsie, The Glory of Living,** Public Theatre, New York, **Second Coming,** Pulse Theatre, New York, **Haremscarem,** Steppenwolf Theatre, Chicago. He is Artistic Director/Founding Member of Hired Gun Theatre Company, Chicago and Artistic Advisor/ Member of Presley Theatre Company, New York.

Bláithín Sheerin *Designer*

Bláithín trained in sculpture and performance art at NCAD and in theatre design at Motley @ Riverside Studios London. Previous work at the Abbey and Peacock Theatres includes **The Sanctuary Lamp, The Morning after Optimism, Bailegangaire, Eden, Made in China, As the Beast Sleeps** and **You Can't Take it with You.** Other designs include **The Comedy of Errors,** RSC, **Our Father,** Almeida Theatre, **The Importance of Being Earnest,** West Yorkshire Playhouse, **Juno and the Paycock,** Lyric Theatre, **The Beckett**

Festival (composite set design), Gate Theatre, John Jay Theatre, New York. She has designed for Druid, Groundwork, Charabanc, Red Kettle, TEAM, The Ark, Second Age and Prime Cut theatre companies. Her designs for Rough Magic Theatre Company include **Midden, The Whisperers, The School for Scandal, Northern Star, Pentecost, The Way of the World, The Dogs, Digging for Fire** and **Love and a Bottle**.

Catherine Fay *Costume Designer*

Catherine is a graduate of the National College of Art and Design. She is the costume designer with Bedrock Theatre Company whose most recent production was **Wideboy Gospel**. She has joined the Abbey Theatre for a year and assisted Joan O'Clery on **Blackwater Angel** and the **Murphy Festival** and she designed the costumes for **Chair** at the Peacock Theatre. Catherine designed costumes for Operating Theatre's **Angel Babel** and has designed for Loose Canon, Corn Exchange, Bickerstaffe, Mandance, Fishamble theatre companies, the Pavilion Theatre and the Gaiety School of Acting.

Tina MacHugh *Lighting Designer*

Previous designs at the Abbey and Peacock Theatres include **The Wexford Trilogy, The Last Ones, Hedda Gabler, The Playboy of the Western World, The Hostage** and **The Hunt for Red Willie**. Other theatre work includes **Shoot the Crow**, Druid Theatre, **Midden, The Whisperers**, Rough Magic Theatre Company, **Sharon's Grave**, Gate Theatre, **A Doll's House, Mother Courage** and **The House of Bernarda Alba**, Shared Experience Theatre, **The Comedy of Errors, Ghosts, Henry VI, The Phoenician Women** and **Shadows**, Royal Shakespeare Company, **Rutherford & Son, The Machine Wreckers** and **Guiding Star**, Royal National Theatre, **Yard Gal**, Royal Court Theatre, **The Colleen Bawn**, Royal Exchange Theatre, Manchester, **The Importance of Being Earnest**, West Yorkshire Playhouse, **The Threepenny Opera** and **Animal Farm**, Newcastle Playhouse, **Our Father**, Almeida Theatre and **Spoonface Steinberg**, Crucible Theatre, Sheffield/New Ambassadors Theatre. Tina was nominated for an Olivier Award for her work on **Ghosts** and **Rutherford & Son**, Opera includes **Il Re Pastore**, Opera North and **Katya Kabanova**, Opera Theatre Company, Dublin, **The Juniper Tree**, Munich Biennale and Almeida Opera Festival, **Idomeneo** and **The Tales of Hoffman**, De Vlaamse Opera, Antwerp, **Der Rosenkavalier**, Scottish Opera and **The Turn of the Screw**, Broomhill Opera at Wilton's Music Hall. Dance credits include work for DV8, Adventures in Motion Pictures, Geneva Ballet, London Contemporary Dance Theatre, English National Ballet, Rambert Dance Company, Houston Ballet, Arc Dance Company, Royal Danish Ballet, Dutch National Ballet and Fabulous Beast, Dublin.

Antoine Byrne *Maeve*

Antoine previously appeared at the National Theatre in **Moving**. Other theatre work includes **A Life**, Olympia Theatre, **The London Vertigo** and **A Month in the Country**, Gate Theatre, **Juno and the Paycock**, Gaiety

Theatre, British tour and West End, London, **The Woman Who Cooked Her Husband,** Cleeres Theatre, Kilkenny, **The Guernica Hotel,** Red Kettle Theatre Company, **The Plough and the Stars,** British Tour, **The Playboy of the Western World,** Second Age and **Angels in America** for 7:84 at the Tron Theatre, Glasgow and the Traverse Theatre, Edinburgh. Film and television work includes **Jumpers** and **Ballykissangel,** BBC, **Kidnapped** and **Oliver Twist,** Disney, **Though the Sky Falls** and **I Went Down.** Antoine also works in radio drama with RTE.

Jason Gilroy *Matt*
This is Jason's first appearance at the National Theatre. He trained at the Gaiety School of Acting. Theatre work includes **Of Mice and Men,** New Theatre, **The Fourth Wise Man,** The Ark, **The River,** Everyman Palace, Cork and the Project, **The Plough and the Stars,** Gaiety Theatre, **Who's Breaking,** Grafitti Theatre Company, **As You Like It,** Druid Theatre, **Cyrano de Bergerac,** Gate Theatre and **Rising of the Moon,** Kilkenny Arts Festival and Dublin Writers Museum. Film, and television credits include **Best, Mystic Knights, Tech TV, The Ambassador, Ballykissangel, Trojan Eddie, Edward No Hands** and **Summertime.**

Brendan Gleeson *Oweney*
Brendan was born in Dublin in 1955. Previously at the Abbey and Peacock Theatres he performed in **King of the Castle, The Plough and the Stars, The Silver Tassie** and **Prayers of Sherkin.** Other theatre work includes **Home, Wasters, Brown Bread** and **Pilgrims,** Passion Machine, **The Cherry Orchard,** Gate Theatre and **Juno and the Paycock** at the Gaiety Theatre which toured to the Chicago Theatre Festival. For the past ten years he has worked in film and television. Recent film credits include **28 Days Later** directed by Danny Boyle, **Plague Season** directed by Ron Shelton, **Gangs of New York** directed by Martin Scorsese, **A1** directed by Steven Spielberg, **Tailor of Panama** directed by John Boorman, **Harrison's Flowers** directed by Elle Chouraqui, **Wild About Harry,** directed by Declan Lowney, **Mission Impossible II** directed by John Woo, **Lake Placid** directed by Steve Winer and **The General** directed by John Boorman for which he won Best Actor at the Boston Society of Film Critics Awards 1998, Best Actor at the 1998 ALFS, Awards of the London Critics and Best Actor at the 1999 ITA, Irish Film and Television Association.

David Herlihy *Eddie*
David is a native of Dublin. His previous work at the Abbey and Peacock Theatres includes **A Whistle in the Dark, Diary of a Hungerstrike, Carthaginians** (Harvey's Award), **Big Maggie, The Silver Tassie, The Countess Cathleen, The Last Apache Reunion, Famine, Asylum! Asylum!, She Stoops to Folly, The Wake** and **The Memory of Water.** Other theatre work includes **Borstal Boy, The Scatterin, The Plough and the Stars, The Risen People,** Gaiety Theatre, **Juno and the Paycock, Les Liaisons Dangereuses, The Dumb Waiter, Long Day's Journey into Night, Arms and the Man,** Gate

Theatre, **I Do Not Like Thee Doctor Fell, Hatchet,** Olympia Theatre, **Macbeth,** Tivoli Theatre, **Anna Christie,** Young Vic, **Three Sisters, The Weir,** Royal Court, Australian tour and Taormina Festival, **Carthaginians,** Hampstead Theatre, **Period of Adjustment,** Palace Theatre, Watford, **The Miser, The Resistible Rise of Arturo Ui,** Royal National Theatre, **The Tower,** Almeida Theatre, London, **The Lament for Arthur Cleary,** Irish Arts Centre, New York, **Dancing at Lughnasa,** US tour, **Translations,** Plymouth Theatre, Broadway and **The Weir,** Walter Kerr Theatre, also on Broadway. On television he appeared in **Glenroe, Echoes, Waterfront Beat, Taggart, Between the Lines, Beck, Making the Cut, The Officer from France, Rainbow's End, Paths to Freedom, The Birthday, Sunday, Reign of Fire, No Tears, On Home Ground** and **Fergus's Wedding.**

Pauline Hutton *Sally*

Pauline trained at the Samuel Beckett Centre, Trinity College Dublin. Previous appearances at the Abbey and Peacock Theatres include **Iphigenia at Aulis, Translations, Give Me Your Answer, Do!, Melonfarmer** and **The Chirpaun.** Other theatre work includes **Midden, The Whisperers,** Rough Magic, Edinburgh Festival, **The Revengers Tragedy,** Loose Canon Theatre Company, **Romeo and Juliet,** Second Age Theatre Company, **The Lonesome West,** Druid Theatre Tour, **Translations,** An Grianan Theatre, **Zoe's Play,** The Ark, Kennedy Centre, Washington, **Tea Set,** a one-woman show written by Gina Moxley and directed by Noeleen Kavanagh. Television and film work includes **Glenroe, This is My Father, Double Carpet, Mad About Mambo, The Closer You Get, Postcards from the Hedge** and a short-cut entitled **Day One.**

Laurence Kinlan *Leonard*

Laurence was born in Dublin. This is his first appearance at the National Theatre. His first role was playing the lead in Alan Bleasdale's drama, **Soft Sand Blue Sea** for Channel 4. He then played Paddy Clohessy in **Angela's Ashes** directed by Alan Parker, appeared in **Saltwater** directed by Conor McPherson, **Everlasting Piece** directed by Barry Levinson, **On the Nose,** directed by David Caffrey and **Country** directed by Kevin Liddy. He appeared in **The Bill** directed by David Caffrey and can be currently seen on RTE's **On Home Ground.**

Frank McDonald *Richie*

This is Franks's first appearance at the National Theatre. His theatre credits include **One Man Show, Uncle Vanya, Hedda Gabler, A Month in the Country, John Gabriel Borkeman, The Buried Child, King Lear, The Tempest, The Merchant of Venice, Macbeth, As You Like It, A Winter's Tale, Henry V** and most recently, **Of Mice and Men.** Films include **Where's Jack, Mackenzie Break, Fistful of Dynamite, The Great Train Robbery, Roses from Dublin, Da, The Field, A Stone at the Heart** and **The Breakfast.** Television credits include **Caught in a Free State, The Irish RM, Making the Cut, The Mannions of America, Hatchet** and Sergeant Cassidy in **The Riordans.**

Amharclann Na Mainistreach
The National Theatre

PERSONNEL

Board
James Hickey (Chairman)
Bernard Farrell
Eithne Healy
Jennifer Johnston
John McColgan
Pauline Morrison
Niall O'Brien
Deirdre Purcell
Michael J. Somers

Artistic Director
Ben Barnes

Managing Director
Richard Wakely

General Manager
Martin Fahy

Director's Office
Ciara Flynn
(P.A. Artistic Director)
Grainne Howe
(P.A. Secretary)

Associate Directors
Garry Hynes
Lazlo Marton
Paul Mercier
Katie Mitchell
Conall Morrison
Lynne Parker
Deborah Warner

Honorary Associate Directors
Vincent Dowling
Tomas MacAnna

Abbey Players
Clive Geraghty
Des Cave

Staff Director
David Parnell

Casting Director
Marie Kelly

Voice Coach
Andrea Ainsworth

Writer-In-Association
sponsored by
Anglo Irish Bank
Jim Nolan

Archive
Mairead Delaney
(Archivist)

Box Office
Adam Lawlor
(Box Office Manager)
Des Byrne
(Box Office Assistant)
Clare Downey
(Chief Cashier)

Box Office Clerks
Catherine Casey
Anne Marie Doyle
Edel Hanly
Lorraine Hanna
Maureen Robertson
David Windrim

Front of House
Pauline Morrison
(House Manager)
John Baynes
(Deputy House Manager)

Cleaning
Joe McNamara
(Supervisor)

Reception
Niamh Douglas
(Senior Receptionist)
Sandra Williams
(Receptionist)

Stage Door
Patrick Gannon
Patrick Whelan

Ushers
Jim O'Keeffe (Chief Usher)
Daniel Byrne
Ruth Colgen
Con Doyle
Ivan Kavanagh
Simon Lawlor
Seamus Mallin
Fred Murray

Education
Sharon Murphy
(Head of Outreach/Education)
Sarah Jordan
(Administrator)
Jean O'Dwyer
(Projects Officer)
Joanna Parkes
(Projects Officer)

Finance
Margaret Bradley
(Financial Controller)
Margaret Flynn
(Accounts)
Pat O'Connell (Payroll)

Literary
Judy Friel (Literary Mgr.)
Jocelyn Clarke
(Commissioning Mgr.)
Orla Flanagan
(Literary Officer)

Press and Marketing
Press Representation
Kate Bowe PR
Katherine Brownridge
(Marketing Manager)
Tina Connell
(Promotions Officer)
Lucy McKeever
(Press & Programmes Officer)

Technical
Tony Wakefield
(Technical Director)
Tommy Nolan
(Production Manager)
Peter Rose
(Construction Manager)
Vanessa Fitz-Simon
(Asst. Production Manager)

Carpenters
Mark Joseph Darley
(Master Carpenter)
John Kavanagh (Deputy)
Brian Comiskey
Bart O'Farrell
Kenneth Crowe
(Assistant)

Scenic Artists
Angie Benner
Jennifer Moonan

Design
Emma Cullen
(Design Assistant)

Electricians
Mick Doyle
(Chief Electrician)
Brian Fairbrother
Joe Glasgow
Barry Madden
Kevin McFadden
(Acting Deputy)

Information Technology
Dave O'Brien (Manager)

Maintenance
Brian Fennell
(Maintenance Engineer)
Tony Delaney (Assistant)

Props
Stephen Molloy
(Property Master)

Stage Managers
John Andrews
Gerry Doyle

Stage Hands
Aaron Clear
Mick Doyle (Fly Master)
Pat Dillon
Paul Kelly

Stage Directors
Finola Eustace
(Head of Department)
John Stapleton
Audrey Hession

Assistant Stage Managers
Stephen Dempsey
Maree Kearns
Nicola Teehan

Sound
Dave Nolan
(Chief Sound Technician)
Cormac Carroll
Nuala Golden

Wardrobe
Joan O'Clery (Acting Wardrobe Supervisor)
Fiona Talbot (Deputy)
Angela Hanna
Vicky Miller
Frances Kelly (Wigs & Hairdressing)
Patsy Giles (Make-Up)

Amharclann Na Mainistreach
The National Theatre

SPONSORS

Aer Lingus
Anglo Irish Bank
Ferndale Films
Dr. A. J. F. O'Reilly
Oman Moving & Storage
RTE
Smurfit Ireland Ltd
Viacom Outdoor
The Irish Times

BENEFACTORS

Aer Rianta
AIB Group
An Post
Bank of Ireland
Behaviour and Attitudes
eircom
Electricity Supply Board
Independent News and Media, PLC
IIB Bank
Irish Life & Permanent plc
Merc Partners
John & Viola O'Connor
Pfizer International Bank Europe
Scottish Provident Ireland
SDS
SIPTU
Unilever Ireland Plc
VHI

PATRONS

J. G. Corry
Brian Friel
Guinness Ireland Group
Irish Actors Equity
Gerard Kelly & Co
McCullough-Mulvin Architects
Mercer Ltd
Smurfit Corrugated Cases
Sumitomo Mitsui Finance (Dublin)
Total Print and Design
Francis Wintle

The Abbey Theatre would also like to thank Guinness Ireland, Heineken and Grants of Ireland.

SPONSORS OF THE NATIONAL THEATRE ARCHIVE

Jane & James O'Donoghue
Sarah & Michael O'Reilly
Rachel & Victor Treacy

FRIENDS OF THE ABBEY

Patricia Barnett
Mr. Ron Bolger
Mrs. Patricia Browne
Ms. Anne Byrne
Mr. Joseph Byrne
Ms. Zita Byrne
Lilian & Robert Chambers
Ms. Orla Cleary
Claire Cronin
Mrs. Dolores Deacon
Paul & Janet Dempsey
Ms. Patricia Devlin
Karen Doull
Paul & Florence Flynn
Ms. Christina Goldrick
Mrs. Rosaleen Hardiman
Sean & Mary Holahan
Mrs. Madeleine Humphreys
Ms. Eileen Jackson
Ms. Kate Kavanagh
Mr. Francis Keenan
Mr. Peter Keenan
Vivienne & Kieran Kelly
Joan & Michael Keogh
Donal & Máire Lowry
Mr. Fechin Maher
Una M. Moran
McCann FitzGerald Solicitors
Ms. Ellie McCullough
Mr. Joseph McCullough
Marcella & Aidan McDonnell
Mr. Liam MacNamara
Dr. Chris Morash
Mr. Frank Murray
Mrs. Mary O'Driscoll
Mr Dermot & Ita O'Sullivan
Mr. Vincent O'Doherty
Mr. Andrew Parkes
Mr. Terry Patmore
Dr. Colette Pegum
Mr. Michael P. Quinn
Mr. Noel Ryan
Breda & Brendan Shortall
Fr. Frank Stafford

ON SUCH AS WE

Billy Roche

Characters

OWENEY
LEONARD
MATT
RICHIE
EDDIE
MAEVE
SALLY

Setting

The stage is divided into three sections.

The main area is a little old-fashioned barbershop – sink, chair, bench, mirror, towels etc. There are two doors – one leading to the hallway, the other to the living quarters.

The second area is the hallway which has a door leading onto the street and a small flight of stairs leading up to the first landing. There are three doors on the landing – one leading to the bathroom, the middle door leading to Matt's bedroom and the third leading to Leonard's room.

The third area is Leonard's room – a lonely little bedsit.

ACT ONE

It is night as the lights rise on LEONARD's *bedsit.* OWENEY, *in his white barbershop coat, is showing* LEONARD *the room.* LEONARD *has a few bags with him. The place is littered with canvas, paintings and easels and paint and brushes etc so that they have to step around the mound of stuff.*

OWENEY. There y'are Leonard. Home sweet home boy! The bathroom and toilet are across the landin' there. Yeh share that with Matt. There's your cooker-bottled gas. Sink. Radiator. A view of the auld hotel and everything free of charge. Sure what more could yeh ask for, hah? (*He forces the window open.*) . . . There's a few fresh sheets and pillowcases there too Leonard. I was goin' to put them on for yeh but then I thought you're probably better at that lark than me so . . . Alright?

LEONARD. Yeah.

OWENEY. I know it's not the Ritz or anythin' but then again you're not Mario Lanza are yeh? . . . Jaysus they're startin' to board up the auld hotel already Leonard, look. It's amazin' how quick they can dismantle everything, ain't it?

LEONARD. Mmn.

OWENEY. Look at P.J. where he is! The Jack Of Hearts, hah! How long were you workin' there anyway Leonard?

LEONARD. In the hotel? I went in there when I was thirteen – straight from St Mary's. I went in as a boots.

OWENEY. And rose up through the ranks, hah! Night Porter Supreme! . . . I'm goin' to tell yeh one thing Leonard but you were queer handy to know boy! (*He calls down to the street and ducks out of sight.*) P.J. . . .

LEONARD *looks a little worried.*

OWENEY (*surfacing*). Look at him. He's too important to look up . . . P stands for prick I think . . . (*He shuts the window.*) . . . Ah well . . . There's the metre for the lights and hot water and all Leonard. Be careful because it'll ate money on yeh. I'm after stickin' a few pound in there just to get yeh goin' and that.

MATT, *the young artist, enters. He looks surprised to see them.*

Matt! Leonard is movin' in here now Matt!

MATT. Yeah?

OWENEY (*his arm around* MATT). Yeah. So you'd nearly need to start shiftin' all this stuff out of his way, like yeh know.

MATT. Where am I supposed to put it?

OWENEY. I don't know Matt. How about your own place, like?

MATT. There's no room over there.

OWENEY. Well hang them on the wall or somethin'.

MATT. None of these are finished yet and I'm sort of superstitious about that.

OWENEY. Yeah well Leonard is a bit superstitious too, like yeh know.

MATT. Yeah?

OWENEY. Yeah. He don't like clutter. (MATT *breaks away.*) That right Leonard?

LEONARD. What?

OWENEY. What are yeh lookin' for anyway?

MATT (*searching through a mound of stuff*). Nothin'.

OWENEY. Huh? . . . Hey I hope you had the good sense to draw a picture of the front of that auld hotel did yeh? 'Cause they're startin' to board it up already.

MATT *disdainfully ferrets out a painting and hands it to him.*

Oh very nice. Do yeh see that Leonard? The front of the
auld hotel. Canopy and all boy! That looks like you,
Leonard. Who's that Matt?

MATT. What?

OWENEY. Is that Leonard?

MATT. Oh I don't know . . . More than likely.

OWENEY. Oon Leonard me boy!

MATT *has found what he was looking for and makes to
leave.*

Here, not to have yeh goin' empty handed or anything.

OWENEY *gives him the painting and gives him another for
his other hand and he stuffs a few more under his oxters
and opens the door for him.* MATT *sighs and leaves.*

Don't be afraid to put the rest of his stuff out on the landin'
at all Leonard. I told him three days ago to shift it. He
pretends not to hear yeh when he don't like what you're
sayin', like yeh know. He pretends not to know me
sometimes. Paid me last month's rent with a paintin'.
The Swan Maiden. I have it hangin' up down below there.
A nice lookin' yoke . . . Mind you, you two'll probably get
on like a house on fire anyway. I'll come up here one day
next week and you'll be sprawled across the bed there
bollock naked and he'll be paintin' your picture or
somethin'.

LEONARD. Yeah?

OWENEY. More than likely. Give us a shout if you need
anything Leonard.

LEONARD. Yeah, right Oweney. Do yeh want me to fix up
with yeh now Oweney or what?

OWENEY. What? No, it's alright Leonard, it'll do when yeh
get on your feet a bit. Unless of course yeh want to pay me
in silverware or somethin'?

LEONARD. What?

OWENEY. I thought I heard a bit of an auld jangle and yeh comin' up the stairs there.

LEONARD. Yeah? (*He puts his hand in his pocket and finds a big bunch of keys.*) . . . Tch . . . The keys of the hotel!

OWENEY. The Phantom Of The Opera, hah! See yeh Leonard.

LEONARD. Yeah, right Oweney and thanks again for everything.

OWENEY *picks up a painting by the door and studies it.*

OWENEY. You're welcome. Oh and listen, cheer up a bit will yeh. I'm your mother now and you can stay out as late as yeh want. This month's rent (*the painting*).

OWENEY *leaves, taking the painting with him.* LEONARD *looks around his lonely room. Lights down. Lights rise on the hall and landing.* OWENEY *raps on* MATT*'s door, lays the painting down and descends the stairs to rummage in the post box.* MATT *appears in the doorway.*

OWENEY (*calling up to him*). This month's rent.

MATT. Yeh what? (OWENEY *indicates the painting.*) . . . Yeah?

OWENEY. Wrap it up.

MATT *thinks about it and sighs.* LEONARD *arrives with a box of* MATT*'s stuff. Embarrassed, he lays it at* MATT*'s feet and hurries back to his room.* MATT *picks up the box and goes back inside. Lights down. Lights rise on the barbershop where* EDDIE *and old* RICHIE *are listening to a boxing match on the radio.* OWENEY *enters, opening a few Christmas cards.*

OWENEY. How's he doin'?

RICHIE. He's gettin' an awful hidin', Oweney. His two eyes are closed and everything.

OWENEY. Yeah?

EDDIE. But sure by right they should have threw in the towel three rounds ago.

RICHIE. He won't lie down all the same.

EDDIE. More courage than sense if yeh ask me. I mean that Coughlan is brilliant.

RICHIE *winces at the radio.* EDDIE *throws a little cluster of punches.*

OWENEY. Keep that guard up Richie.

RICHIE. What's that?

OWENEY. . . . Anyone lookin' for me?

EDDIE. Yeah, that Mrs Whatshername was here lookin' for yeh. Corcoran.

OWENEY. Huh?

EDDIE. She said yeh gave her son a queer lookin' haircut the other day here. She came in to fleece yeh.

OWENEY. I gave him what he asked for – a Mohican.

EDDIE. Yeah well yeh picked the wrong tribe then. She looks more like a Maw Maw to me. She said you're lucky his da is away at sea or he'd've been down here after yeh.

OWENEY *shrugs it off.*

OWENEY. What can yeh do? . . . I was just sayin' to Leonard up there that they've started to board up the auld hotel already.

EDDIE. But sure that place is practically gutted inside. I was in there today to get the auld grandfather clock out of it. I had to take it up to P.J.'s place.

OWENEY. I see P.J. ramblin' around there earlier on alright – surveyin' his kingdom!

EDDIE. Yeah? Fair play to him. Yeh should see the house he has though lads. Out of this world boy! And he has everything in it.

RICHIE. I'd say that.

EDDIE. Every gadget under the sun.

RICHIE. Go away.

EDDIE. Oh yeah. No shortage there.

OWENEY. Is he happy though?

EDDIE. He looks fairly fuckin' happy to me anyway. His missus is after openin' that little boutique across the street there yeh know. He's not that happy about that mind yeh.

RICHIE. No?

EDDIE. Oh no. Did yeh ever see her Oweney?

OWENEY. Yeah, she's headin' this way now.

EDDIE. What?

OWENEY. I thought she'd get here sooner or later. Women can't resist a barber shop. Reminds them of their da or somethin'.

MAEVE *enters.*

MAEVE. How are yeh? Is Eddie here? . . . Oh Eddie.

EDDIE. Yeah?

MAEVE. Them young fellas are around the back again Eddie. They're throwin' stones and I'm afraid of my life they'll break a window or somethin'.

EDDIE. Alright, I'll hunt them out of there for yeh.

OWENEY. Any excuse boy!

EDDIE. Huh?

MAEVE. What's that?

EDDIE. Nothin'.

OWENEY *chuckles.*

MAEVE. What?

EDDIE. Don't mind him.

EDDIE *leaves.* MAEVE *stays.*

OWENEY. Alright?

MAEVE. Yeah . . . I'm Maeve by the way. The little shop across the street there.

OWENEY. Oh right . . . 'Maeve's' yeh mean?

She nods.

MAEVE. And you're Oweney, right?

She points to him and he places his fingertips to hers and makes the hissing sound of electricity.

OWENEY. No gloves? (*He warms her hands.*) . . . What do yeh think?

MAEVE. What? (*He indicates the place.*) . . . Lovely.

She moves around the shop, touching things etc, stopping to admire a photograph.

OWENEY. Me, me da and me grandda. Three generations of scalpers. We improved from generation to generation I think though, didn't we? Hah? I mean . . .

He presents himself.

MAEVE. I don't know! (*He chuckles.*)

OWENEY. That's my family there. That's Sharon. My oldest girl. Derek is twelve. Carol – she's six. And that's Pauline – me missus. Well . . . used to be . . . How's P.J.?

MAEVE. Alright. Do yeh know P.J.?

OWENEY. I went to school with him.

MAEVE. Oh, right. You're not the fella who sat in the desk beside him by any chance, no?

OWENEY. Not if I could help it, no. Mind you if I'd've known he was goin' to own the whole neighbourhood someday I'd've sat on his lap.

MAEVE. Well not the whole neighbourhood Oweney. He doesn't have your place yet?

OWENEY. All he has to do is ask . . . How's business over there anyway?

MAEVE. Alright. Well a bit slow to start with like but . . . alright I suppose. Not fast enough for P.J. of course.

OWENEY. Yeh have some fairly good-lookin' women goin' in and out. Little Tommy Day was takin' his life in his hands here this mornin' askin' me for a shave. What are yeh sellin' over there anyway?

MAEVE. Oh yeh know – the usual. Dresses, tops, lingerie.

OWENEY. Yeah? Well if yeh ever need anyone to do any measurin' up or anything.

She chuckles.

MAEVE. I'm disturbin' that man now. (RICHIE *has turned off the radio.*) . . . Eddie is after roundin' them up. What's he doin', tryin' to catch them or somethin'? I was only wantin' him to whatdoyoucallit . . .

OWENEY. Don't worry he won't catch them fellas.

MAEVE. He's inclined to be a bit heavy-handed sometimes I think.

OWENEY. Mmn . . . Who are they anyway? Young Flynn. I'll have a word with them tomorrow for yeh.

MAEVE. Thanks Oweney. The old neighbourhood, hah!

OWENEY. Yeah.

MAEVE. P.J. was tellin' me that he used to play handball up against that gable wall one time.

OWENEY. We did everything against that wall – handball, rounders, taws. All the different seasons. And do yeh see that auld shore there. Malachy Morris got drunk for the first time and lost his false teeth down that shore. We opened it up and hauled them out and stuffed them back into his mouth.

MAEVE. Aw Oweney!

OWENEY. We dragged him home then between us – little Tommy Day singin' the theme to Mister Ed. A horse is a horse! . . . He looked like a horse! . . . This was a good

street then though yeh know – a great street. Looks like a
wasteland now I know but . . . there was gold out there that
time . . . Mmn . . .

Pause.

MAEVE. I'd better get back. You're workin' late!

OWENEY. So are you.

MAEVE. Stocktakin'. Anything but go home.

OWENEY. That's how it starts yeh know. P.J. was around there
earlier on.

MAEVE. Yeah? I didn't really want him to know about the
young lads. Yeh might tell Eddie not to say anything will
yeh.

OWENEY. Yeah, right.

MAEVE. P.J. thinks I'm made of sugar I think. I'll see yeh
Oweney. Thanks for the tour . . . Oh and listen if he wants
to buy this place don't sell it to him. Right?

OWENEY. Right!

She peeps out and slips away. OWENEY *watches her go.*

RICHIE. He's after givin' up the ghost Oweney.

OWENEY. Huh?

RICHIE. He's after throwin' in the towel.

OWENEY. Yeah? . . . I'll throw in the towel meself I think
Richie. (*He takes off his shop coat and hangs it up.*) How's
the missus Richie?

RICHIE. I don't know to tell yeh the truth Oweney. I haven't
been able to get up to see her for a few days now. Eddie
was supposed to drop me up to the auld nursin' home this
afternoon but something came up for him he said and he
just couldn't make it. I don't like not seein' her, like yeh
know, 'cause she's not that happy up there.

OWENEY. She don't like it, no?

RICHIE. She do not. She sort of blames me for puttin' her in there in the first place but sure what could I do. I mean I just couldn't manage her, like yeh know.

OWENEY. Sure I know.

EDDIE *enters.*

EDDIE. Oweney, are you goin' for a pint later on or what?

OWENEY. Yeah I'm just goin' to make meself a cup of tea and have a bit of a wash and then I'm goin' over.

EDDIE. Right. (*He admires himself in the mirror.*) I'm goin' to tell yeh one thing but that little Flynn fella'll be gettin' the greatest slap in the gob off of me one of these days – havin' me chasin' him like that!

OWENEY. Go away they're only young fellas, you're worse!

EDDIE. Yeah, right. (*He smells his armpits.*) . . . I'll see yeh over there. I have to go and pay the bould Tommy Day a bit of a social call.

OWENEY. Yeah? What for?

EDDIE. Would yeh believe he still hasn't come up with P.J.'s money?

OWENEY. Why, how much does he owe?

EDDIE. That's not the point Oweney. The point is he still hasn't come up with it.

OWENEY. Yeah but what does he owe yeh though?

EDDIE. It's not me, it's P.J.

OWENEY. What does he owe – thirty, forty, fifty, what? (*He reaches for his wallet.*)

EDDIE. Who do you think you are, eh? – the Mother Of Sorrows or someone?

OWENEY. All I'm askin' is how much does he . . .

EDDIE. This has nothin' to do with you.

OWENEY. But sure where's the point in whatdoyoucallit . . .

EDDIE. Look money or no money he's goin' to get a slap
anyway so . . . forget it

OWENEY. Huh?

EDDIE. Forget it. Put your money away and forget it. I'll see
yeh over there.

EDDIE *exits.*

OWENEY. Where's the point in that? I mean little Tommy
Day, like! Yeh know – singin' and dancin' and all.

RICHIE (*rising*). Eddie is what we used to call in the auld days
a bum, Oweney. And I know I'm supposed to be his uncle
and all but . . . a bum's a bum no matter what way you look
at it . . . She's shuttin' up shop, hah!

OWENEY. Huh? (*He goes to the window.*) . . . She's lovely
boy.

RICHIE. She's a nice lookin' woman alright. My missus
looked a bit like her in her day yeh know.

OWENEY. Yeah?

RICHIE. In her day she did, yeah.

OWENEY. You were lucky then Richie.

RICHIE. I suppose I was . . . See yeh Oweney.

OWENEY. Night Richie . . . She is lovely though.

RICHIE (*in the hall*). Oh now.

RICHIE *leaves.* OWENEY, *smitten, gazes out the window.*
Lights down. Lights rise on the bedsit. It is morning.
LEONARD *is sitting on a chair while* MATT *stands behind*
his easel, painting a portrait of him.

LEONARD. The nun brought us all down to the picture house
to see *The Ten Commandments.* We were marched through
the town in twos. I was holdin' me little sister's hand so
tight I must have been nearly hurtin' her. But I was afraid of
my life I was goin' to lose her, like yeh know. In me own
hometown! Anyway some of the local lads started jeerin' us
as we were standin' in the queue – callin' us names and that.

I tried to explain to one of them that meself and Bernadette shouldn't really be in St Mary's at all – that our Mammy and Daddy were still alive – but he wouldn't listen to me. They let us into the picture for half price, put us sittin' in the hard seats. They might as well have put a big placard around our necks. Even to this day I still can't buy anything for half price. The gas thing about it all though is that no one saw the funny side to it. I mean bringin' a crowd of orphans to a picture that began with a woman rollin' her baby down a river in a basket.

LEONARD *chuckles.*

MATT. Mmn . . . So what exactly happened anyway? You woke up one mornin' and your mother was gone?

LEONARD. Yeah.

MATT. What age were yeh?

LEONARD. I was seven. Bernadette was five. I knew straight away that we were in trouble. I mean I knew we weren't goin' to be able to pull out of it that easy or anything. Me da started drinkin' then and six months later we were taken into care.

MATT. And did he go up to see yez and all?

LEONARD. Yeah, he used to come up most Sundays, like. But he was usually half jarred and that. In the end he more or less stopped comin' altogether.

MATT. Do yeh drink yourself?

LEONARD. No.

MATT. Why not? Afraid you'll end up like him or somethin'?

LEONARD *shrugs.*

Huh? . . . Did she ever come back?

LEONARD. No.

MATT. Yeh never saw her again? (LEONARD *shakes his head.*) Mmn . . . It's queer though ain't it? A woman abandonin' her young like that . . . Mind you I suppose there's worse things than being alone in the world.

(*He lights up a cigarette and turns on the radio.*) . . . That'll do for today. I'm gettin' tired.

MATT *covers up the painting with a cloth and turns towards the window.* LEONARD *sits there, feeling like a stranger in his own place. Meanwhile* MAEVE *has been making her way up the stairs to knock on* MATT*'s bedroom door. On receiving no reply she turns to rap on* LEONARD*'s door.* LEONARD *rises and goes to answer it.*

MAEVE. I'm lookin' for Matt . . . Oh . . . We talked yesterday Matt about me buyin' some of your paintings for the shop.

MATT. Huh? Oh, right . . . I'll eh . . .

A little flustered, MATT *stubs out his cigarette and searches frantically for his coat and then he leads her across the landing to his own room.* LEONARD *takes a tiny peek in at the painting. Lights down. Lights rise on the barbershop.* EDDIE *is having his hair cut.* RICHIE *is sitting on the bench, reading a magazine.*

RICHIE. Jaysus that was fairly rough about that Titanic though lads wasn't it?

EDDIE. What's that?

RICHIE. Huh?

OWENEY. . . . . Tommy Cooper where he is!

EDDIE. Take it easy now Oweney – don't scalp me or anythin'.

OWENEY. Sit still will yeh. You're goin' bald in the back too, I don't mind tellin' yeh.

EDDIE. What? Where?

OWENEY. In the back. Grey as well as bald, hah! You'll be a hunt!

EDDIE. Show us.

OWENEY crosses for some hair lotion. EDDIE takes a small mirror and holds it up to the light while he looks at himself in the big mirror.

OWENEY. I hope you're goin' to take this man here out to see your poor Aunty Cissy this afternoon are yeh?

EDDIE. Hah? No I can't. I've too much to do. That's only me scalp.

OWENEY. What can yeh do Richie?

RICHIE. That's what I say. I mean it's only fourteen miles but she might as well be on the moon as far as I'm concerned.

LEONARD (*entering*). I'm goin' now Oweney.

OWENEY. What? Oh yeah, right Leonard. Yeh know what to do now don't yeh?

LEONARD. Yeah I think so. What do I say to her again though?

OWENEY. Just tell her you're wantin' to make a claim. See Mary Whatshername . . . Healy. She knows yeh anyway. Have yeh got your P45 and all the rest of it?

LEONARD. Yeah, I have everything I think.

EDDIE. Where's he goin'? – the dole office?

OWENEY. Yeah.

EDDIE. Aw! (*Goes to him.*) . . . Are yeh alright?

LEONARD. Yeah.

EDDIE. You look a little nervous and there's no need to be yeh know.

LEONARD. No, I'm not nervous.

EDDIE. Are yeh sure?

LEONARD. Yeah.

EDDIE. That's good. Have yeh got money and all?

LEONARD. Yeah, I have money.

EDDIE. Have yeh? Give us a loan of a fiver will yeh?

LEONARD. What?

OWENEY. Leave him alone will yeh.

EDDIE. What? (*He pretends to hit* LEONARD.) . . . Here, hold that. Higher (*the mirror*). . . . That's it. That's only me scalp Oweney. Hold it steady will yeh. Yeah. Everyone has that. Anyway yeh can't have hair and brains can yeh? Hah?

LEONARD. What's that?

EDDIE (*mocking*) What's that!

SALLY *enters, wearing a red beret and a red overcoat with a scarf tied around her neck like an air hostess. Under her coat she wears a bright coloured dress. She radiates lonesomeness.*

RICHIE. Here she is now lads. Shorthand typist extraordinaire!

OWENEY. Huh?

EDDIE. Things are lookin' up lads.

SALLY. What's that supposed to mean?

EDDIE (*mocking again*). What's that?

EDDIE *laughs and sits back into the chair and* OWENEY *applies the hair lotion and combs his hair etc.*

RICHIE. Are yeh lookin' for me Sally?

SALLY. Yeah. Sister Angela wants to know where did yeh put the key to the big shed.

RICHIE. What do she want that for?

SALLY. I don't know. Her high nelly bike or somethin', I suppose.

RICHIE. Oh right. It's in the vestibule in the big earthen jar tell her. But sure I'll be up there tomorrow afternoon anyway.

SALLY. Right.

OWENEY. I thought you were supposed to be finished up there altogether Richie?

RICHIE. Ah I just do the odd auld day up there now – now and again, like yeh know. But sure most of the children are gone out of there now. Green beans and onions Oweney that's what I'm reduced to . . . Do yeh recognise this fella Sally? One of the old boys! (*Indicates Leonard.*)

SALLY. Yeah? Ain't it well for him to be out of it?

RICHIE. But sure you won't be long more there now Sally, will yeh?

SALLY. I will not. I'll be gone out of there before Christmas so I will.

RICHIE. Ah you'll surely see the Christmas out there now Sally?

SALLY. I will in me hat. Sure why would I? If I got a job.

RICHIE. Well this fella here misses the place like anything he tells me. That right Leonard?

LEONARD *scoffs.*

SALLY. I'd say that.

RICHIE. What?

LEONARD. I don't miss the smell of cocoa anyway I can tell yeh. I hates the smell of cocoa boy!

RICHIE. Yeah – cocoa and sticky buns, hah! Sally McEvoy – Leonard Carroll.

SALLY. Oh I heard of you. Your escapade over the wall and all.

LEONARD. What?

RICHIE. He was a divil.

LEONARD. But sure I only went out to get me little sister's ball, like yeh know.

RICHIE. Yes, a divil yeh were boy!

LEONARD *titters.*

LEONARD. Sister Una bet the lard out of me over that boy.

OWENEY. Yeh paid the price Leonard, hah?

LEONARD. Yeah.

RICHIE. Oh someone always has to pay the price boy. How's little Bernadette?

LEONARD. Alright. She's livin' in England now. Slough. Workin' in a hotel over there she is.

RICHIE. Yeah? . . . Tch . . . Jaysus you did more mindin' on her – fair play to yeh. Poor little Bernadette! . . . Sister Una though Leonard, hah! Jaysus she was one ugly woman lads. Wasn't she Leonard? Admit it now. A face that'd stop a clock man! She's workin' up in the hospital now I believe – turnin' stomachs!

Laughter.

EDDIE. Well Sally – at any more carnivals lately, no? (*He pays* OWENEY.)

SALLY. What? . . . No.

EDDIE. Hah?

Silence.

SALLY. I've to go. I've to meet a few people up the town. See yeh Richie.

RICHIE. Yeah right Sally – see yeh tomorrow.

OWENEY. All the best Sally.

SALLY *stares into* LEONARD's *sad eyes and leaves.* EDDIE *primps.*

RICHIE. She's a nice-lookin' girl lads, ain't she? Hah? Caused a fair bit of a stir up there from time to time too I don't mind tellin' yeh. Sister Veronica had to put her on the pill and everything there last year I believe.

OWENEY. Yeah?

RICHIE. Oh yes, the brave Sally dragged the lot of them kickin' and screamin' into the twenty-first century so she did. And wasn't she right?

OWENEY. I suppose.

EDDIE. Oh it has to be fed lads and it won't ate hay.

Laughter. MAEVE *is standing in the doorway, a few paintings in her hands.*

MAEVE. Can I see yeh for a minute Oweney?

OWENEY. What? . . . Yeah, right . . . Unisex!

He follows her out to the hall. Lights down on the shop. Lights rise on the hall.

OWENEY. What's up?

MAEVE. Matt tells me your heart is sort of set on this picture here.

OWENEY. Yeah it is. Why?

MAEVE. Huh? . . . No it's just that I'm wantin' to buy a few of his paintings for the shop and that's me in the background there yeh see.

OWENEY. Yeah I know. That's what I'm wantin' – a faraway picture of you.

MAEVE. Yeah?

OWENEY. Yeah. Well I mean you hardly want to buy a paintin' of yourself anyway do yeh?

MAEVE. No? . . . No, I suppose not.

She gives him the painting.

OWENEY. What else have yeh got there? Oh yeah, I like that one. The front of the small hotel. The auld canopy and all.

MAEVE. The Square looks real kind of whatdoyoucallit . . . Parisian or somethin' don't it?

OWENEY. Yeh think so?

MAEVE. Yeah – sort of. Well yeh know in a whatdoyoucall-it . . . roundabout sort of way, like.

OWENEY. Mmn . . .

LEONARD (*entering*). I'm off now Oweney.

OWENEY. Oh yeah, right Leonard. Good luck. Yeh know what to do now don't yeh?

LEONARD. Yeah. Mary Whatshername . . . Healy. Right?

OWENEY. Yeah. And whatever yeh do don't mention my
name to her.

LEONARD. No? Why not?

OWENEY. Go ahead will yeh . . . (LEONARD *leaves*.) . . .
Leonard! That's him there by the way (*in the painting*).

MAEVE. Yeah? Oh yeah, it is too. He looks like he has a
hump on his back there.

OWENEY. That's just the weight of the world. He's fairly
good though ain't he?

MAEVE. Matt? Yeah, he's very good. I'm thinkin' of gettin'
him to do something special for me sometime – a close-up
picture of you maybe, hah?

OWENEY. Yeah, right. Then you'll have a close-up picture of
me and I'll have a faraway one of you.

MAEVE. Yeah . . . right . . .

OWENEY. Yeh know where you're goin' now don't yeh? Just
turn left of that auld Eiffel Tower there!

She slaps him playfully and leaves. He watches her go.
EDDIE *enters.*

EDDIE. What have yeh got there? Huh? (*He looks at the
painting and then at* OWENEY *who is miles away.*) Don't
even think about it.

OWENEY. What?

EDDIE. You know what.

EDDIE *exits up to the bathroom.* OWENEY *gazes lovingly
across the street again. Lights down. Lights rise.* MATT *is
sitting on the top step of the landing.* SALLY *is knocking on*
LEONARD*'s bedsit door.*

MATT (*rolling a joint*). He's not there. He's gone out.

SALLY. How long is he gone?

MATT. Early this mornin'. He's gone on some kind of expedition.

SALLY. Huh?

MATT. Flask and sandwiches and all.

SALLY. What time will he be back at?

MATT. He didn't say. I didn't ask.

SALLY. Is that dope you're smokin'?

MATT. Yeah. Are yeh wantin' some?

SALLY. No thanks.

MATT. No? . . . Hey weren't you goin' to be some sort of a nun one time or somethin'?

SALLY. No.

MATT. I thought you were. One time, no? . . . Mmn . . . Pity. I'd like to defrock a nun now.

SALLY. Not the ones I know yeh wouldn't.

MATT. Yeah but there's bound to be a couple of fairly good lookin' ones too though ain't there?

SALLY. Yeah – one or two I suppose. Rita Bryne is fairly good lookin'. She was goin' to be a nun one time but . . . then she didn't.

She is sitting on the step beside him now. He takes a firm hold of her face and examines it.

MATT. Would you like to pose for me sometime?

SALLY. What, naked yeh mean?

MATT. Not necessarily.

SALLY. I don't know . . . I'll see.

MATT. Mmn . . . To tell yeh the truth, I'm not mad about paintin' naked women anyway. I mean I don't want to end up like a doctor or anything. Yeh know, too used to it or somethin'. Do yeh know what I mean?

SALLY. Mmn . . .

EDDIE *enters, slightly high on something.*

EDDIE. Well, what have we here? Two lonely people together!
(*He sings.*)

I Fell In Love With You . . .

Not to worry. Uncle Eddie is here now. Do yeh know what
I'm sayin'? Do yeh know where I'm comin' from? Do yeh
know where I'm goin' to? Do yeh know where I want to be?
Huh? Hah? What's that? Do I detect a slight hint of
whatdoyoucallit in the air? I do. Give me a blast of that
there will yeh – before I suffocate. Oh yes, that's good shit.
Where did yeh get this stuff – till I break his fuckin' legs . . .
So what were you two talkin' about there anyway before I
so rudely whatdoyoucallit . . . Huh? Love? Aw! That's nice.

He sings:

And The Last Waltz Could Last Forever.

Yeh know if I could paint like you – which I can't – but if
I could I'd paint a picture of you two on the stairs there
now. Two Lovers On The Stairs, I'd call it. By Eddie
Dunwoody. I'd change me name to Dunwoody 'cause he's
my favourite jockey and I know how to ride. That right
Sally? (*He sings.*)

Got Myself A Crying, Talking, Sleeping, Walking,
    Living Doll.
Got To Do My Best To Please Her Just 'Cause She's
    A Living Doll.

*He dances his way up and down the stairs and catches a
glimpse of himself in the mirror.*

Careful Eddie, gettin' a bit of a paunch there. Still! You two
take care there now you hear me and if anyone bothers you
you just call on Eddie Dunwoody Jones – 24137654321

EDDIE *primps his way into the barbershop where* RICHIE
is sitting beside the radio. OWENEY *is by the window.
'Holy Cow' is on the radio.* EDDIE *sings along and dances
around to the tune with little silly chicken-like movements.*

EDDIE (*sings*).
>I Can't Eat. I Can't Sleep.
>Since You Walked Out On Me.
>Holy Cow What You Doing To Me . . .

The song fades out and the D. J. begins.

D.J. That was 'Holy Cow' there from Lee Dorsey. After this break we'll be talking to P.J. Dawson – well-known local property developer and entrepreneur and all-round good guy . . . But first . . . (*an ad break*).

EDDIE. P.J.'s on the radio.

OWENEY. Turn that thing off there Richie will yeh. It's bad enough havin' to look at that fella hangin' around the street all day without havin' to listen to him on the radio too.

RICHIE *turns it off.*

EDDIE. Hey . . . Hey . . .

OWENEY. All round good guy me bollix! I mean that fella is ruinin' this street.

EDDIE. Hey . . . Hey . . . Hey . . .

OWENEY. I mean just think about it Richie. The corner shop is gone. The shoe shop is gone. Bill Bailey's Bar is gone. And now he has the auld hotel too.

EDDIE. Hey . . . Hey . . . Hey . . . Hey.

OWENEY. And what's he puttin' in their place? Monstrosi-fuckin'-ties that's what! Sure did yeh see what he did to Boyle's house? And if it stopped there we might be alright but it don't. And it won't either.

EDDIE. Hey . . . Hey . . .

OWENEY. The Jack Of Fuckin' Hearts goin' around !

EDDIE *has his arm around his neck now and gazes fawningly into his eyes.*

Yes, the Jack Of Hearts! . . . I'm only speakin' the truth and if the truth hurts then it's not my fault.

EDDIE. What's wrong with yeh? Hah? Huh? What's up?
Come on, tell your uncle Eddie all about it.

OWENEY. What's up? I'll tell yeh what's up. I've had three
customers all mornin' that's what's up. And one of them
didn't pay me 'cause he hadn't any money on him. I'll see
yeh when I get me glasses he said.

EDDIE. Do yeh want me to sort him out for yeh? Hah? No? . . .
Here, have a Mother's Little Helper. Cheer yeh up a bit.

OWENEY. Go away from me will yeh. The last time I took
one of them I nearly shaved a fella's beard off by mistake.

EDDIE (*popping a pill*). Suit yourself . . . Why don't yeh go
see P.J. anyway?

OWENEY. What for?

EDDIE. You know what for? P.J.'s dyin' to get his hands on
this place.

OWENEY. He'll be waitin' then.

EDDIE. But sure where's the point in that when there's no one
comin' in and out of here. Take the money and run I say. Set
yourself up on the Mall or somewhere. That right Richie?
Oweney's Rendezvous!

OWENEY. Look, let's get this straight, I'm a barber not a
poncey hairdresser – back-combin' and blow-dryin' and all
the rest of it. Do me a favour will yeh.

EDDIE. Yeah that's alright Oweney but . . . I mean meself and
Richie come in here because we don't care what our hair
looks like but most people do yeh see.

OWENEY. What's that supposed to mean?

EDDIE. Well yeh have to admit Oweney you're a little bit
whatdoyoucallit sometimes – old fashioned.

OWENEY. I'm not a little bit old fashioned at all. I am old
fashioned and proud of it. My da had this place before me
and his da before him and I'll be straight about it – I'm
hopin' my young lad'll take it over after me.

EDDIE. That's not goin' to happen Oweney. I mean take a good look around yeh boy. Take a good look out that window there. Richie, what are yeh lookin' at me like that all the time for?

RICHIE. What?

EDDIE. With those big sad eyes and all?

OWENEY. He's lookin' at yeh because you were supposed to bring him up to see his missus this evenin'. Yeh promised.

EDDIE. I can't drive a car in my condition. I mean it'd be irresponsible of me. Is that what you're wantin? Me to be irresponsible – knock a child down or somethin'! A few days before Christmas! I mean I can't believe you fellas sometimes. Yeh know. I mean . . . Jesus . . . And another thing you'll be gettin' yourself killed over that one too.

OWENEY. What one?

EDDIE. What one! . . . I know you're mad about her and all the rest of it but the way you're goin' on is ridiculous altogether so it is!

OWENEY. I'm not mad about her. I just like lookin' at her that's all,

EDDIE. That hasn't gone unnoticed. Any milk in it?

EDDIE *has poured himself a cup of tea and goes into the living quarters to look for milk.*

OWENEY. What did yeh do about little Tommy Day after?

EDDIE (*off*). Nothin'. I couldn't find him. He's gone into hidin' on me.

OWENEY. But sure why don't yeh just let me pay the money for him and be done with it?

EDDIE (*off*). Now don't start that Anthony Of Assisi crap again.

OWENEY. What? . . . Anthony of Assisi!

RICHIE. I'll go Oweney.

OWENEY. Yeah right Richie.

RICHIE. How much would it be to hire a taxi Oweney?

OWENEY. It'd be too dear Richie.

RICHIE. Would it? I thought that alright.

OWENEY. If I had a car meself I'd drop yeh up there no bother.

RICHIE. Sure I know that Oweney. No quicker man.

OWENEY. Leave it with me anyway. I'll see if I can think of someone.

RICHIE. Alright . . . I hates not seein' her, like yeh know.

OWENEY. I know. That other fella should have dropped yeh up that far anyway.

RICHIE. But sure he has his own life to live I suppose. It's just that I'm sort of runnin' out of time with her, yeh know . . . I'll see yeh Oweney.

OWENEY. Yeah right Richie, see yeh . . . Don't worry about it. We'll think of somethin'.

RICHIE *exits.* EDDIE *enters, sniffing a carton of milk.*

EDDIE. I don't know if this is alright or not. Me uncle Richie gone, yeah?

OWENEY *throws him a dirty look.*

. . . What? . . . Look I forgot, right! Is that alright with yeh? If I forgot! I couldn't bring him today anyway 'cause I have to go to Enniscorthy in a minute – to see a dog about a cat. To tell yeh the truth I thought he'd be glad to see the back of her by now. 'Cause she gave him a dog's life yeh know. Sure she ran away on him and everything one time. He had to go over and bring her back. Tiger Bay or somewhere. No biscuits, no? (*He sings.*) Love Is A Many Splendour Thing . . . Did Richie say there was somethin' about the Titanic in one of these?

EDDIE *sits on the bench and thumbs his way through some magazines.* OWENEY *plonks himself down on the barber*

*chair. Lights down. Lights rise on the barbershop. It is
night.* OWENEY *is making a pot of tea.* MAEVE *is sitting
on the bench, eating chips.*

MAEVE. I'd say he was glad to get up and see her all the same
though would you?

OWENEY. Who? Richie? Oh yeah. Although he said she spent
most of the time with her face to the wall. She just can't
seem to forgive him for puttin' her in there in the first place.
But sure what could he do? I mean he just couldn't manage
her any more, like yeh know.

MAEVE. Aw!

OWENEY (*bringing her the tea*). Thanks for bringin' us up
there by the way.

MAEVE. No problem. I'll drop ye there anytime Oweney.
Sure it's only up the road really.

OWENEY. Yeah I know but still . . .

MAEVE. Seems to be a nice enough place.

OWENEY. The nursin' home? Yeah. There's a lovely little wood
close by it too. I'll take yeh in there the next time we're up
there – while we're waitin' for him. (*She chuckles.*) . . .
What?

MAEVE. Nothin' . . . Where have yeh got my picture hangin'
by the way?

OWENEY. Beside me bed! Would yeh like to see it?

She slaps him playfully.

MAEVE. They were lovely (*the chips*) . . . I was starvin'. I
didn't eat anything all day, like yeh know.

OWENEY. Busy?

MAEVE. Yeah – a little. Although P.J.'s not too happy with the
takin's. He never wanted to give me the shop in the first
place of course. He wanted to turn it into a fast-food joint or
somethin'. I'm not coddin' yeh before he's done this little
Square'll be all whatdoyoucallit . . . neon!

OWENEY. The neon man, hah!

MAEVE. Mmn . . . (*She crosses to put her chip paper in the basket.*) He gets on my nerves though yeh know – askin' me how much I took in all the time . . . Yeh should see the plans I have for the place though Oweney. Pine shelves all along the walls with the stuff all sparsely laid out on 'em and all. And a real avant-garde counter in the middle of the shop – yeh know, a round one. And a little coffee bar in the corner. Flowers and paintings and ornaments all over the place. Yeh know I think I can make it really nice yeh know. Unusual! . . . If I'm let of course. Is that one of Matt's?

OWENEY. What? (*She indicates a painting on the wall.*) . . . Oh yeah. The Swan Maiden. Last month's rent. It seems a wounded swan swam into town one day and got tangled up in the wild reeds, and when a man came to her rescue she turned into a beautiful woman in his arms. He fell in love with her and he married her and he hid her wings away so she could never leave him. While he's not lookin' though she goes out searchin' for them – traipsin' through the meadow and down by the river and all – longin' to be off.

MAEVE. Oh yeah. There they are there in the long grass – just out of reach. Her reflection in the water is a swan Oweney, look. Did yeh see that? That's very clever . . . (*She moves to a photograph.*) . . . Your da was a fairly handsome man wasn't he? You must follow your mother do yeh?

OWENEY. God blast yeh anyway.

MAEVE *giggles as she tries on his white shop coat.*

MAEVE. P.J. has no photographs of the old days at all – yeh know his communion and confirmation and all the rest of it. I mean what does that tell yeh? Somethin'! What do yeh think? (*She presents herself.*)

OWENEY. A good lookin' barber.

MAEVE (*tapping the chair and spinning it*). Next.

OWENEY *crosses to the chair. She covers him with a sheet and pretends to snip his hair with a scissors and brush him down etc.*

MAEVE. That's a grand class of a day now. Were yeh up at the match, yeah?

OWENEY. Match?

MAEVE. Yeah? No?

OWENEY. Yeh what?

MAEVE. Did yeh say yes or no? Was that yes yeh were or no yeh weren't? Shave? . . . Bum be bum be bum . . .

She lathers him up and attempts to shave him with a cut-throat razor. She finds it awkward to manoeuvre. He guides her onto his lap. She settles herself and proceeds.

MAEVE. Am I doin' it right?

OWENEY. Oh yeah. This is exactly how I shaved little Tommy Day the other day here now . . . The face of yeh!

MAEVE. Stay quiet will yeh.

OWENEY. Huh?

She tries to scrape away the hairs with her fingers and she blows on his face to see how she is doing. He takes her by the hand and, holding the razor at bay, he kisses her softly through the shaving foam. Pause.

MAEVE. Mmn . . . That's enough of that I think.

She rises.

OWENEY. You're not supposed to leave a man with half a beard.

MAEVE. And you're not supposed to kiss the barber.

OWENEY. I couldn't help it. I was under the influence.

MAEVE. Of what?

OWENEY. Eh . . . You.

MAEVE (*tossing him a towel*). What's in there?

OWENEY (*wiping the foam from his face*). My room.

MAEVE. Oh! . . . Right . . . The Mohican, hah! (*A photograph.*)

OWENEY. Huh? . . . Oh yeah, young Corcoran. I did that yeh know.

MAEVE. I know. I was in the crowd sure.

OWENEY. Yeah, a big crowd gathered round the shop and everything. I was like Salvador Dali or someone! Probably get me lynched of course but . . . that's what he wanted.

MAEVE. Young fellas, hah!

OWENEY. Mmn . . . I never saw you out there.

MAEVE. I was incognito . . . (*She looks at herself in the mirror.*) I'd say she was fairly good lookin' when she was young yeh know . . . Richie's wife? You can still see the ghost of it there somewhere – when yeh look close. (*She shudders and turns away.*) . . . What kind of a haircut did you want when you were a young lad? Wild I suppose?

OWENEY. Real neat, I was a bit of a mod, like yeh know. Dancin' to little Tommy Day and the boys. (*He sings and dances.*)

I've Been Told When A Boy Meets A Girl.
He Takes A Trip Around The World.
Hey Hey Bop Chew Wha Bop Bop Bop
Chew Wha Hey Hey Bop Chew Wha
Bop Bop Bop Chew Wha . . .

MAEVE (*dancing about*).
Bop Bop Chew Wha Bop Bop Bop Chew Wha . . .

OWENEY. Hey Hey Now Mama. That's What I Say.

MAEVE. Bop Chew Wha Bop Bop Bop Chew Wha . . .

OWENEY. They'd slow it right down then and you'd wrap yourself around some young one. The Answer To Everything or somethin' . . .

MAEVE.
Bop Chew Wha. Bop Bop Bop Chew Wha . . .

OWENEY (*sings*)
Don't Ask Me A Mountain Of Questions . . .

MAEVE. And yeh took all your girls back here I suppose did yeh?

OWENEY. One or two of them, yeah – when me da wasn't lookin'. In fact this is where Pauline told me the bad news. Over there somewhere. (*He sings.*)

Do You Love Me, Really Love Me, As I Love You?

Sad pause.

MAEVE. Why did yeh leave your family Oweney?

OWENEY. I didn't. Pauline put me out.

MAEVE. Why, what did yeh do?

OWENEY. Oh I don't know. Ramblin' and gamblin' and stayin' out late at night and all.

MAEVE. Yeh still see them though don't yeh?

OWENEY. Oh yeah – all the time. Although my oldest girl Sharon is still not talkin' to me. She turns away or crosses the street whenever she sees me comin' now. Which is a bit awkward because the young lad wants me to spend Christmas Day with them, like yeh know, and Pauline said that might be alright but Sharon insists you won't stay there if I come so . . . I don't really know what to do.

MAEVE. I asked P.J. one time if he'd like to have children someday and he just shook his head . . . Do you wear glasses Oweney?

OWENEY. For readin', yeah. How about you?

MAEVE. Who wants to know?

OWENEY (*chuckles*). I'd like to see you with glasses now. Nothin' else, just glasses.

She laughs, puts on OWENEY'*s glasses and struts.*

MAEVE.
    Bop Chew Wha Bop Bop Bop Chew Wha . . .

Pause.

OWENEY. Pauline's seein' someone else now yeh know. I saw the two of them crossin' the Square the other day there, holdin' hands. Although she says it's just platonic but . . . I don't know. All of a sudden she's a bit of a mystery to me again.

MAEVE. I used to think P.J.'s silence meant he was mysterious but I'm not so sure any more now . . . I hate that house Oweney. It's like livin' in a fortress I swear – alarms and cameras and all the rest of it. He says there's a limit to the time I can keep the shop too, that if I don't make a go of it fairly soon he's goin' to take it back from me. He thinks that'll stop me but it won't. 'Cause I want to do somethin' Oweney, yeh know. I want to be someone – in my own right! Yeh know? Not just attached to someone else all the time. I know that probably makes me sound like a bit of a bitch and all but I don't care . . . Mind you, I'll probably only be gettin' on my feet when he'll want to move again. 'Cause he never stays put. When he's here he wants to be there. When he's there he wants to be somewhere else. And he wants to knock everything down – the house where he was born in case somebody sees it, the old hotel for spite, the whole neighbourhood if necessary. Anything but stand still. Sure we had a lovely little orchard at the back of the house and he tore it down to build a poolroom. And he don't even play pool like! . . . I mean I don't really know anyone any more Oweney, yeh know. I mean I've no real friends or anything. And I'm not sayin' it's all P.J.'s fault or anythin'. It's not. It's mine. I mean I'm probably not whatdoyoucallit . . . I don't know . . . likeable or somethin'!

OWENEY. Of course you're likeable . . . Well I like yeh anyway.

MAEVE. Yeah but do yeh though Oweney, or do yeh just like what yeh see, like?

OWENEY. Oh no I hate what I see . . . Ah . . . Lort . . . Hah? (*He pretends to spit, etc.*)

MAEVE (*going to him*). Do yeh know what I mean though Oweney?

OWENEY. Yeah I know what yeh mean but the grass is wet.

MAEVE. What?

She pretends to slap him. He takes her in his arms and draws her to him and she snuggles into him.

MAEVE. Oh you . . .

OWENEY. Oh you yeh mean!

They kiss.

MAEVE. We shouldn't be doin' this Oweney.

OWENEY. Yeah I know but I'm sort of gone though, yeh know. And you know I am too. Watchin' yeh movin' around the boutique and slippin' across to the little coffee shop and all. If I was a painter I could paint your picture but I'm not. I was half thinkin' of tyin' yeh up and runnin' away with yeh sometime – to Donegal or somewhere. Demand twenty thousand ransom and when P.J. comes up with the money I'd refuse to take it.

MAEVE. Mmn . . . that's nice.

OWENEY. Yeah? Which part? Donegal or the ransom?

MAEVE. Paintin' my picture.

She turns around and he wraps his arms around her from behind as she sinks deeper into him. LEONARD *enters, carrying a couple of Christmas trees.*

LEONARD. Sorry Oweney, I didn't know that you were whatdoyoucallit . . .

OWENEY. What? . . . Shit . . . (*They disentangle.*) . . . Leonard.

SALLY (*from the shadows on the landing*). Leonard!

LEONARD. Yeah?

SALLY. What kept yeh?

LEONARD. What?

SALLY. I've been waitin' for yeh.

LEONARD. Have yeh? . . . Oh right . . .

She spies the Christmas trees and comes down the stairs.

SALLY. Deadly! . . . Are one of these for your place, yeah?

LEONARD. Yeah.

SALLY. Which one? . . . This one. (*She peeps into the shop at* MAEVE *and* OWENEY.) . . . Give us the key.

Sally sings.

Santa Claus Is Coming To Town . . .

She goes back up the stairs with the Christmas tree and lets herself into the bedsit, much to LEONARD*'s alarm.*

LEONARD. I have a Christmas tree for yeh Oweney.

OWENEY. What? . . . Where did yeh get that?

LEONARD. I hitched up to Enniscorthy today because I heard there was a job goin' in Murphy-Floods Hotel.

OWENEY. Yeah? How did yeh get on?

LEONARD. It was already gone before I got there. But the manager was very nice about it. He knew me and all the rest of it, like yeh know. He said it was a pity I didn't come up yesterday because he definitely would have considered me for the job. Anyway on the way back Eddie picked me up and he stopped at a field and knocked off four Christmas trees – one for himself and his ma and one each for you and me. He just jumped out of the car with a hacksaw and hopped in over the fence. I had to keep nix for him.

OWENEY. Bonnie and Clyde, hah!

LEONARD. I was goin' to give yeh the other one Oweney – it's a handy little one – but . . .

OWENEY. Huh?

LEONARD. Jaysus your man Eddie is mad though ain't he? Hah?

OWENEY. Mmn.

OWENEY *and* LEONARD *are out in the hall now.*

SALLY (*off*). Leonard.

LEONARD. Yeah right, I'll be up there in a minute. You don't mind Oweney do yeh?

OWENEY. No. Par for the course here Leonard. Women.

LEONARD. So I see. Although I wouldn't say Matt is too handy with them would you? Hah?

OWENEY. He wouldn't be in our calibre Leonard. Alright Sally?

SALLY (*on the landing*). How are yeh.

LEONARD *goes up the stairs.* OWENEY *watches them as they go inside. He goes back to the shop.*

OWENEY. I forgot all about him . . . Are you wantin' that tree for the shop?

MAEVE. No, I've a white one ordered.

OWENEY. A white one, hah!

MAEVE (*taking off the shop coat*). I'd better get out of here Oweney. He won't say anything will yeh? P.J.'d go mad if he heard about this.

OWENEY. It's alright, he won't say nothin'.

MAEVE. What about her?

OWENEY. She won't say anythin' either.

MAEVE (*putting on her coat.*) Let's hope not. 'Cause P.J. hears everything, like yeh know.

OWENEY. Am I goin' to see you again?

MAEVE. I only work across the street sure.

OWENEY. That's not what I mean.

She chuckles in exasperation.

MAEVE. Oh I don't know Oweney. Let's just wait and see, hah – play it by air. I mean my life is complicated enough as it is without whatdoyoucallit . . .

OWENEY. Complicatin' it!

MAEVE. Yeah.

OWENEY. O.K.

Slight pause.

MAEVE. I would like to see that little wood sometime though yeh know.

OWENEY. Yeah?

MAEVE. Yeah. (*She takes his hand.*) Walk through the woods in the rain with yeh sometime, hah! . . . Better go, eh?

OWENEY. Yeah. Are yeh alright now?

MAEVE. Yeah, I'm calm now.

OWENEY. That's good. Go ahead then.

MAEVE. Right. (*She moves to the door.*) . . . Thanks Oweney.

OWENEY. What for?

MAEVE. Ah, yeh know . . . It gets a bit cloudy for me sometimes yeh know.

OWENEY. I know.

Pause. She leaves. OWENEY *looks down at the Christmas tree and sighs. Lights down. Lights rise on* LEONARD'*s room.* LEONARD *is bent over the fire, raking it back into life as he whistles, 'I Once Loved A Sailor Boy.'* SALLY *is rummaging in a bag.*

SALLY. I have a few things for yeh. A coal fire and all though, hah! It's lovely.

LEONARD. Huh?

SALLY. This is for above your door (*a Brigid's cross*). To watch over yeh. Mistletoe for over your bed – for good luck and fertility. A few sprigs of holly for above your fireplace. Not to go up anywhere in the house until Christmas Eve – 'cause it's very bad luck . . . I'll leave the holly here, look . . . (*She gets a chair and proceeds to put the Brigid's cross above the door*.) . . . Yeh know I think you've probably found a real friend in that other fella down there, yeh know.

LEONARD. Who's that? Oweney?

SALLY. Mmn . . . I mean I know people say he's a bit of a chancer goin' around and all and I suppose he probably is at heart but at the back of it all yeh know I'd say he's probably alright. Not like that Eddie fella anyway. I can't abide that lad. Thinks he's God's gift or somethin'. I like a fella to be sort of shy or somethin', yeh know.

LEONARD. Oweney's not shy.

SALLY. You, I mean.

LEONARD. What? . . . Oh, right.

He moves to the stove, whistling the song again.

SALLY. When I move into my own place I'm goin' to have a coal fire too. And bare floorboards on the floor with a load of big rugs all over the place. And I'll have one of those big old-fashioned quilts on the bed. All my hats'll be hanging on the wall opposite – one for every mood. I'm goin' to live above an old grocery shop or somewhere. Awake every morning to the smell of coffee and fresh bread and all.

LEONARD (*making the tea*). Yeah?

SALLY. Yeah. There'll be flowers out on the landing and an old crock of a bike in the hall and I'll go off ridin' through the town every day – with me big summer dress on me.

LEONARD. Even in the winter?

SALLY. It'll be summer all the time then.

LEONARD. I hope it keeps fine for yeh.

SALLY. It will.

LEONARD. A coal fire in the middle of the summer though – you'll be sweltered.

She laughs and moves to the covered-up easel.

SALLY. What's this? (*She uncovers it and gasps.*) . . . Huh? . . . What have yeh got it covered up for?

LEONARD. Matt don't want me lookin' at it all the time. He's superstitious about it or somethin'.

SALLY. But sure how would he know?

LEONARD. He senses it he says. (*He takes her a cup of tea.*) Got a rake of hats then have yeh?

SALLY. No, not yet but I will when I'm workin'. I'm not so sure he captured the essence of you in that now.

LEONARD. Huh? . . . (*He covers up the painting.*) What do yeh hope to work at anyway?

SALLY. I don't know. In an office or somethin'.

LEONARD. Can yeh type, yeah?

SALLY. A hundred words a minute . . . I know that song.

LEONARD. Huh? . . . (*She hums.*) . . . Maureen Benson's song.

SALLY. Huh?

LEONARD. Maureen Benson. She used to work in St Mary's laundry. A big girl with a red face – always laughin'. She married a fella from Glynn. He was a bread man. They had a dose of children too I believe.

SALLY. And did she live happily ever after, yeah?

LEONARD. Not really.

SALLY. I heard Carol Kelly singin' that. She's always singin' that.

LEONARD. But sure they used all be singin' that song up there. I had a pain in me face listenin' to it to tell yeh the truth.

SALLY. Yeh should hear Carol Kelly singin' it then, you'd have a pain in your arse. I'm not coddin' yeh she makes a right auld come-all-ye out of it. She sings through her nose all the time. And she looks like a dolphin. Yeh know her face is all sort of whatdoyoucallit . . . caved in like.

LEONARD. Oh I know who you're talkin' about now. Is she still there? She must be nearly due a pension out of that place by now.

SALLY. She took meself and poor Rita Bryne into the orchard one night yeh know. Rita thought she was pregnant and Carol said that she might have a spell that could cure it for her and she took an apple and she wrote some magic words on it and she told Rita to eat it, heart and all.

LEONARD. What did she write on it?

SALLY. I don't know. Latin or somethin'.

LEONARD. Did it work?

SALLY. She never had a baby anyway.

LEONARD. Mmn . . . Maureen Benson was supposed to have a cure for a scald. Three Ladies From The East or somethin' . . . What room have they got yeh in anyway?

SALLY. The attic.

LEONARD. With the whatdoyoucallit . . . protrudin' windows and all?

SALLY. Yeah.

LEONARD. That was Bernadette's room. They wouldn't let the two of us sleep in the same room so every night after dark I used to have to climb out onto the roof and go down to her and stay with her until she fell asleep. There's a great view of the town from up there though yeh know. All the auld streets and all. I used to be queer tempted to steal away some night and go down to my own house – feck a few Goldgrain biscuits for the two of us or somethin'. (*He chuckles.*)

SALLY. Mmn . . . I like that room mind yeh. Up beside the moon there . . . It's startin' to snow Leonard, look . . . Rita Bryne is workin' in a solicitor's office now yeh know. She says she loves it. (*She sings softly.*)

I Once Loved A Sailor Boy
He Told Me He'd Always Be True

When He Swore By The Stars Up Above Me
He Looked A Lot Like You.

He Promised He'd Buy Me A Pretty White Dress
With Ribbons Of Gold And Of Blue
Then He Bade Me Farewell In The Morning
And He Looked A Lot Like You.

Do Do Do Do Do Do Do Do Do Do Do Do Do Do. . . .

I don't know the rest. Do you know the rest?

LEONARD (*recites*).
Is He Out On The Indian Ocean
Or The Rivers Of Old Illinois
As He Sails 'Neath The Stars Up Above Me
My Handsome Young Sailor Boy.

Pause. She kisses him and touches his face.

SALLY. I'm goin' to have to come down and look after you
I think.

LEONARD. You're goin' to look after me?

SALLY. Yeah. Why, what's wrong with that?

LEONARD. Nothin'.

SALLY (*taking his hand*). I'm just wantin' you to promise me
one thing, that if you're goin' to let me down you'll do it
nice and easy.

LEONARD. Let yeh down! What do yeh mean let yeh down?
I'm not goin' to let yeh down,

SALLY. What?

LEONARD. Jesus Sally I'm the one who's whatdoyoucallit
here yeh know . . . I mean . . .

SALLY. Shh . . .

LEONARD. I'm not goin' to let yeh down though, yeh know.

SALLY. Yeah well, we'll see.

LEONARD. What?

She kisses him again and, turning to look out at the falling snow, she lays her body into his.

LEONARD (*wrapping his arms around her from behind*).
I won't let yeh down.

SALLY (*sings*).
Is He Out On The Indian Ocean
Or The Rivers Of Old Illinois
As He Sails 'Neath The Stars Up Above Me
My Handsome Young Sailor Boy.

Lights down. Lights rise on the barbershop. RICHIE is standing by the window. MAEVE is standing close by. MATT is sitting on the bench, sketching. A few sketches lie about the place. It is late afternoon.

MAEVE. They're lovely Matt.

MATT. Huh? They're just a few rough sketches.

MAEVE. Mmn . . . they're lovely. Oweney where he is though, hah. I think I recognise this fella too. The Jack Of Hearts!

She holds up one of the sketches.

MATT. Yeh what?

Awkward pause. OWENEY enters from the living quarters.

MAEVE. I'm just sayin' here Oweney, you've a right little hive of activity here haven't yeh?

OWENEY. Oh yeah we get 'em all in here – actors, singers, comedians and all. If only one or two of them'd spend a few bob now I'd be right. Is that any good to yeh? (*He hands her a plumber's plunger.*)

MAEVE. Yeah, that should do the trick alright. I'll give it a shot anyway. I'll be over to collect Richie then – as soon as I shut the shop.

OWENEY. Yeah, right. Did yeh hear that Richie? Maeve'll be over to collect yeh as soon as she shuts the shop.

RICHIE. Oh, right. Thanks missus.

OWENEY. I won't be able to go with yeh today because I've another Mohican comin' at five. I've started a trend apparently.

MAEVE. Salvador Dali, hah!

OWENEY. Yeah. Salvador Dali, Picasso and whatshisname . . . Legs Diamond.

MAEVE. What does that make me?

OWENEY. I don't know. Venus in blue jeans or someone.

MAEVE. Old Mother Hubbard'd be more like it. I'll see yez. Thanks Oweney.

OWENEY. Yeah, right Maeve.

RICHIE. All the best.

OWENEY (*following her out to the hall*). Oh Maeve.

MAEVE. Yeah?

OWENEY. I wasn't too heavy the other day here or anythin' was I?

MAEVE. Yeah, yeh were. You were like Jack The Ripper here.

OWENEY. Was I? . . . No I wasn't though was I?

MAEVE. My lips are sealed. (*She holds the plunger to her mouth and exits.*)

Pause. OWENEY *returns to the shop.*

RICHIE. What did she say to you again Oweney?

OWENEY. She said she's shuttin' up the shop early this evening and she'll drop yeh up that far.

RICHIE. And how will I get home?

OWENEY. She'll wait for yeh I suppose. Or call back for yeh. One of the two. Who are you drawin' Matt – him or me?

MATT *indicates* RICHIE.

OWENEY. Try and look a bit anguished there Richie will yeh.

RICHIE. What's that?

OWENEY. I say he likes to see a bit of agony in his pictures, don't yeh Matt?

MATT. Mmn.

RICHIE. No shortage of that then!

OWENEY. They're lookin' good Matt.

MATT. They're just a few sketches . . . I'd like to really capture the heart of this place though Oweney yeh know. Yeh know the smell of it and the sound of it and all. I'd like someone to look at the paintin' and nearly know what song was playin' on the radio at the time.

OWENEY. The More I See You, hah! (*He sings.*)

The More I See You. The More I Want You . . .

MATT. Yeh know what I mean though Oweney?

OWENEY. Yeah but the grass is wet though Matt.

MATT. Huh? . . . I mean I want to paint a picture of that old man there now right and I want everyone to know the whole story. He's an old man who waitin' for a lift to take him to the hospital to see his wife who's dyin' a little bit every day on him. And all the regrets and whatdoyoucallits – incriminations and all – are etched on his face. Yeh know? A whole lifetime of them!

OWENEY. Mmn.

MATT. It's queer hard though yeh know.

OWENEY. Yeah, well . . . it would be . . . They're good . . . Do she know you're comin' up Richie?

RICHIE. Yeah I rang up there this mornin'. The nurse says she's still very down in herself. She wants to come home but sure . . . She thinks I'm payin' her back for somethin' or somethin' yeh know.

OWENEY. Yeah? What?

RICHIE. Oh I don't know. Somethin' or other.

MATT. Yeh see that's what I mean now. That's exactly what I
mean . . . But it's impossible to whatdoyoucallit, like yeh
know . . . I mean . . . Oh I don't know.

MATT *tears out the page in despair and rolls it into a ball,
throws it away and starts again.* LEONARD *enters.*

LEONARD. I got this this mornin' Oweney.

OWENEY. Huh? What is it?

LEONARD. It's a summons. Someone saw me with the
Christmas trees.

OWENEY. Who?

LEONARD. Some fella ridin' by on a bike. He recognised me
from the hotel seemingly.

OWENEY. Show us.

LEONARD *gives him the summons.* OWENEY *puts on his
glasses to read it.*

RICHIE. Are they takin' yeh to court Leonard?

LEONARD. Yeah. Christmas Eve.

RICHIE. Over a Christmas tree?

LEONARD. Yeah. Well four of them like. A cop nabbed me
this mornin' on the corner there. He tried to get me to tell
him who the fella with me was but I said nothin'.

RICHIE. There was a fella with yeh?

LEONARD. Yeah. Eddie. I wouldn't mind but I didn't even
want a tree in the first place.

RICHIE. What do it say Oweney?

OWENEY. It's just a summons like.

RICHIE. That's bloody scandalous so it is. Fellas sellin' drugs
and everything else and they're comin' after him for
knockin' off a few auld Christmas trees.

OWENEY. But sure what can they do to him anyway only fine
him. I mean they're not goin' to send him to jail or anything.

RICHIE. Well no but . . . nevertheless.

LEONARD. But sure it's me first offence, like yeh know . . .
Would yeh say I'd need a solicitor Oweney?

OWENEY. I don't know Leonard. I suppose so. Better to have
one anyway.

EDDIE *enters.*

OWENEY. Did yeh see this Eddie? Leonard is after gettin' a
summons for the Christmas trees.

EDDIE. When?

OWENEY. A cop nabbed him on the corner there this mornin'
he says.

EDDIE. Well I hope yeh didn't mention my name to him did
yeh?

LEONARD. No, I never said nothin'.

EDDIE. No and you're not to either. That's all I need now.
Six months in Mountjoy or somewhere for knockin' off
a few auld Christmas trees. I'd be the laughin' stock of
the place up there. So whatever yeh do don't mention my
name, right. Leave me out of it. And I don't care if he has
yeh by the balls leave me out of it. Right? He's a fuckin'
jinx that fella is Oweney. I mean how long have I been
gettin' us Christmas trees every year? – ten, eleven years
now! And most of them out of that field too. I bring Mao
Tse-Tung along once and the whole shebang comes
crumblin' down around me. I don't know. A fuckin' jinx
yeh are boy!

LEONARD. My only concern now Oweney is that this might
go against me when I'm lookin' for a job or somethin'.

OWENEY. Naw you'll be alright Leonard.

LEONARD. It'll probably go in the paper though Oweney.

OWENEY. Yeh might be lucky.

LEONARD. Huh?

EDDIE. There's always the underworld. Although on second
thoughts maybe not . . . I got two hundred smackers for yeh
Oweney.

OWENEY. What?

EDDIE. For the paintin' of the queer one across the street . . .
P.J.

OWENEY. I'm not sellin' that picture.

EDDIE. Come on now Oweney and have a heart. I got yeh
over the odds for it.

OWENEY. How do yeh make that out?

EDDIE. How do I make that out? . . . Matt how much are you
payin' for that kip of a room yeh got upstairs there – a
month now?

MATT. One-twenty.

EDDIE. One-twenty. You're makin' eighty quid just like that
and I'm not even takin' a drink for meself out of it.

OWENEY. You're all heart Eddie.

EDDIE. I am, ain't I?

OWENEY *turns away.*

. . . Look Oweney I'll be straight with yeh. P.J. don't like
the idea of a gobshite like you havin' a painted portrait of
his missus hangin' on your bedroom wall, like yeh know.
And I can't say that I blame him either.

OWENEY. He'll get used to it.

EDDIE. I don't think so somehow or other. What's the point
anyway? I mean you can hardly even make her out in it.

OWENEY. I wouldn't expect you to understand Eddie.

EDDIE. You're the one who don't understand Oweney. Yeh see
P.J. sent me to talk to you about this. Yeh know? P.J. – me –
you. Yeh know?

OWENEY. Huh?

EDDIE. I mean he could have sent anyone but he didn't. He sent me. He could have asked big Hank Whatshisname Thomas to come and you'd be on the floor by now. But he didn't Oweney. He sent me. Do yeh know what I'm gettin' at? It's a test. He's testin' me. Yeh know? For somethin' big like!

OWENEY. What's the name of this picture you're in Eddie till I try and rent the video of it some night.

EDDIE. That's very funny Oweney but P.J. sent me and I think you know what that means.

OWENEY. Yeah I heard about little Tommy Day.

EDDIE. Big Hank gave Tommy a couple of slaps, yeah.

OWENEY. He put him in the hospital is what I heard.

EDDIE. Look forget about Tommy Day. Tommy Day is nothin'.

OWENEY. Tommy Day is Tommy Day!

EDDIE. He's a song and dance man who forgot how to dance.

OWENEY. He's Tommy fuckin' Day!

EDDIE. From the candy store on the corner for Christ's sake. I mean do me a favour will yeh.

OWENEY. It don't matter he's still Tommy Day and if a fella like that can't walk around owin' someone a couple of quid then what's it all about. I mean he did his bit. He paid his dues.

EDDIE. But sure who knows Oweney maybe he'll end up forgin' a whole new career for himself out of this – yodellin' through a straw or somethin'!

OWENEY. You tell P. J. that picture's not for sale.

EDDIE. That's not what he wants to hear Oweney. I mean you know P.J.

OWENEY. Yeah I know P.J. I went to school with him. Look at him sideways in the yard and he'd run home and tell his granny on yeh.

EDDIE. So yeh don't want this money then? . . . Oweney, Oweney, Oweney, you're puttin' me in a very awkward position here. I mean what am I supposed to say to this man? 'Cause he's right outside there in the car yeh know.

OWENEY. Tell him the picture's not for sale and neither am I. And if he don't like it he can come in here and bite my arse.

EDDIE. You want me to tell P.J. to come in here and bite your arse.

OWENEY. With mustard on it if he likes.

EDDIE. With mustard?

OWENEY. Whatever he likes.

The phone is ringing.

EDDIE. Now that'd make a right picture.

MATT. What?

EDDIE. Answer that will yeh (*the phone*).

LEONARD. What? . . . Oh yeah, right.

EDDIE. Fair enough . . . How's me Aunty Cissy, Richie?

RICHIE. Much the same Eddie.

EDDIE. Yeah? . . . Ah sure that's the way it goes.

EDDIE *steps towards* OWENEY *and hits him in the stomach.* OWENEY *goes down on one knee.*

EDDIE. Better I caught yeh unawares Oweney. If you knew it was comin' you'd've only tightened up on me and I'd've cracked a rib on yeh or somethin'. Are yeh alright? Try and straighten up now . . . That's it. Go over to the window Oweney . . . Now you're learnin' . . . Where's the paintin'? – down in the room? Yeah? . . . Answer it will yeh! (*The phone.*)

EDDIE *disappears into* OWENEY's *room.* RICHIE *comes to help* OWENEY. LEONARD *answers the phone in the hall.*

LEONARD. Hello . . . Yeah . . . He's a bit tied up at the moment. Who's calling please? . . . Oh right Pauline. Hang on . . .

EDDIE (*enters with the painting*). I'll leave your money here Oweney. Look. Alright? I don't know what you're makin' such a fuss about anyway; you can hardly even make her out in it.

RICHIE. I'm goin' to tell yeh one thing but if I was a younger man I'd take you outside and I'd sweep the street with yeh so I would.

EDDIE (*titters*). Me uncle Richie where he is! . . . (*He goes to* MATT.) And listen here you, in future you pay that man his rent in hard cash. Never mind your paintin's. Yeh can't eat a paintin' yeh know and that man has a wife and family to support. So in future you pay him in cash and be done with it. And don't tell me yeh haven't got it either. You get the dole and your rent allowance the same as the rest of us. So hand it over. 'Cause if I find out that you haven't paid him his rent I'll come up there and wreck the place on yeh and I'll throw you out through the fuckin' window. Yeh fuckin' little prick yeh! Don't go makin' a big deal out of this now Oweney . . . (*He goes to* LEONARD *in the hall.*) . . . You wanted a loan of a hundred. P.J. said yes. But first I want to know what you want it for?

LEONARD. I'm wantin' to buy Sally a decent Christmas present.

EDDIE. Yeah? Do yeh want to wrap this up for her?

LEONARD. What?

EDDIE. Huh? . . . Yeh know she's goin' to let yeh down don't yeh? Sooner or later! As soon as yeh turn your back. Yeh know that don't yeh?

LEONARD. What? . . . No, she's a nice enough girl!

EDDIE. Yeah, right . . . Here and don't spend it all in the one shop. And remember when I come lookin' for this you better have somethin' for me. Right? . . . It's better this way Oweney. Better for you, better for me, better for everyone.

Anyway – faraway women and all the rest of it Oweney yeh know. Faraway women boy!

EDDIE *exits.*

MATT. I'm goin' to tell yeh one thing Oweney but if I'd've known that that fascist bastard was goin' to get his hands on my paintin' I never would have gave to you in the first place. And to make matters worse you end up makin' money out of it. Well I'll make a bonfire out of my work before I see that happenin' again boy. 'Cause I'd sooner dig ditches now than that.

MATT *gathers his things and exits.*

LEONARD. It's for you Oweney . . . Pauline . . . Hang on Pauline.

OWENEY *goes to the phone and sits on the bottom step of the stairs.*

OWENEY. Pauline . . . Nothin'. I'm a bit out of breath that's all. Mmn. So what's the story? Christmas dinner? No? Why not? Oh right . . . Well what mass is Sharon goin' to? Maybe I could come up while she's at mass or somethin'. Midnight mass. What Christmas Eve yeh mean? What time is midnight mass startin' at? Half ten! But sure I'll come up while she's at midnight mass and see the lads before they go to bed.

RICHIE. That's a right cur that fella is Leonard.

LEONARD. What's that?

OWENEY. But sure they'll hardly be asleep by then Pauline. What time are yeh puttin' them to bed at? Half nine. Will Sharon be still there at that time? She will.

RICHIE (*exiting*). Yes, a right cur goin' around he is! . . . I don't know where we got him out of at all.

OWENEY. Well look why can't yeh keep them up until half ten or somethin'. Well when am I supposed to see them for Christ's sake. Yeah I know that Pauline. You don't have to keep remindin' me all the time. No, you were the one who . . . Pauline you were the one who decided not me . . .

Anyway, look, I don't want to get into that right now . . .
Alright, look, we'll figure out somethin'. Did Derek give
yeh the envelope? There's an extra hundred in there just
to . . . Mmn

MAEVE *enters.*

I don't know . . . I don't know what I'll do. Stay here I
suppose . . . But sure what else can I do? I mean . . .
Mmn . . . Yeah right. See yeh.

He hangs up the phone.

MAEVE. What's goin' on Oweney?

OWENEY. How do yeh mean?

MAEVE. P.J. just arrived with the paintin'. I thought yeh said
you wanted to hang on to that?

OWENEY. Yeah I did but . . . I sort of changed me mind about it.

MAEVE. Yeah? How come?

RICHIE. I'll be with yeh in a minute missus.

MAEVE. Yeh what?

RICHIE. I'm just wantin' to . . . (*He indicates the bathroom.*)

MAEVE. Yeah right Richie . . . Take your time . . . So what
happened? P.J. offer yeh over the odds for it or somethin'?

OWENEY. Somethin' like that.

MAEVE. Oh, right. So much for paintin' my picture and all
the rest of it.

OWENEY. Yeh what? (*She sighs and turns away, disappointed.*)
. . . It's a pity I can't go with yeh now. This Mohican yeh
know.

MAEVE. Don't matter.

OWENEY. I was wantin' to show yeh the little wood though
yeh know.

MAEVE. Never mind. The way things are goin' it'll probably
be sold off and built on before we get there anyway. Tell
Richie I'll wait in the car for him.

OWENEY. Yeah, right Maeve.

She exits.

LEONARD. What will I do about this summons Oweney?

OWENEY. Oh for Christ's sake Leonard what am I, your fuckin' mother or somethin'?

LEONARD. What?

Pause. OWENEY *slumps down in the chair, holding his aching stomach.* LEONARD *sadly leaves, mounting the stairs to his own room.* RICHIE *passes him on the stairs and exits.* OWENEY, *alone in the shop. Lights down.*

ACT TWO

Lights rise on the bedsit. LEONARD *is adjusting his tie in front of the mirror. The place is somewhat dismal looking. There is no fire lighting in the grate, the bed is unmade and the Christmas tree still lies lopsided and undecorated in the corner.* MATT *enters.*

MATT. What's goin' on?

LEONARD (*putting on his coat*). How do yeh mean?

MATT. Where are yeh goin'?

LEONARD. I'm up in court today.

MATT. Tch.

LEONARD. Why, what's up?

MATT. Well I was goin' to try and finish off that paintin' this mornin'.

LEONARD. But sure I'll be back later on like. Some of the lads were sayin' that the judge probably won't let it go on too long anyway because of the day that in it, like. And who knows with a bit of luck I might get called first, hah?

MATT. I'll be gone by then. I'm goin' to go out home for Christmas.

LEONARD. Yeah? That's nice Matt.

MATT. Do me a favour will yeh. Balloons and party hats and all the rest of it. I mean they haven't a clue.

LEONARD. Well it is Christmas Matt.

MATT. I know it's Christmas for Christ's sake but do we have to go through the same rigmarole all the time. I mean the same rigmarole year in and year out. I mean, come on.

Don't they know the depths that some of us have to go to every day – every minute of every day! Don't they realise? I tell yeh somethin' for nothin' but you're better off the way you are, believe me.

LEONARD. How do yeh mean?

MATT. To have no one belongin' to yeh to annoy yeh or anything.

LEONARD. I have.

MATT. Huh?

LEONARD. But sure I've a sister livin' in England, like yeh know.

MATT. Yeah well . . . I may try and finish this by memory now and I hate doin' that.

LEONARD. Sorry Matt.

MATT turns to unveil the painting.

Oh if Sally calls while I'm out yeh might ask her to hang on here for me till I get back, will yeh? . . . I'll see yeh then Matt, eh.

MATT. Mmn.

LEONARD. Oh . . . (*He gives* MATT *a Christmas card.*) . . . Happy Christmas.

MATT. What? . . . Yeah . . . right.

LEONARD leaves. Pause. Lights down. Lights rise on the barbershop. OWENEY *comes out of the living quarters, drinking tea and shaving with an electric razor. The Christmas tree is glittering in the background.* LEONARD *comes down the stairs, stops in the hall and considers rapping on the door. He changes his mind, stuffs a card under the door and leaves.* OWENEY *draws back the curtains and lets the blind up on the door. He picks up the card as* RICHIE *enters with some newspapers.*

RICHIE. There y'are Oweney – *The Irish Times* and *The Independent. The Daily Mirror* is not in yet she says.

OWENEY. Oh, right Richie. Thanks.

RICHIE. Physician heal thyself, hah!

OWENEY. Mmn . . . Is that alright? (*He feels his stubbled chin.*)

RICHIE. Grand.

OWENEY. It'll do says you . . . Leonard (*the card*).

RICHIE. I see him goin' up the street there – atin' an apple. And the condemned man had a hearty breakfast, hah!

OWENEY. What? . . . Oh that's right, he's up in court today ain't he? I forgot all that. I meant to whatdoyoucallit . . . How did he look?

RICHIE. A little concerned to me but then I suppose he would wouldn't he? Thank God for the Probation Act says you ! . . . But sure as he said himself it's his first offence.

OWENEY. Yeah . . . What are you goin' to do today?

RICHIE. Eddie is goin' to drop me up to the auld nursin' home in a few minutes. He's just eh . . . You don't mind Oweney do yeh?

OWENEY. Mind? No, why?

RICHIE. Oh I don't know. Yeh know? . . . To be honest I was very nearly goin' to tell him to stick his lift up his hole but then I thought hang on now Richie – there's no point in cuttin' off your nose to spite your face or anything.

OWENEY. You're right too Richie. Take it while it's goin', I say. To tell yeh the truth the two hundred pounds came in handy after. I had to buy Derek a walkie-talkie and it cost me a hundred and twenty. I mean I know I'll probably have a fairly good day today and all but I was a bit stuck for cash at the time, like yeh know.

RICHIE. A hundred and twenty pounds! God be with the days, hah! An auld plastic knife or a little toy gun or somethin'. Or a spinnin' top one year I got.

OWENEY. Yeh wouldn't be givin' them spinnin' tops now Richie. Unless of course it was electric or somethin' and aligned to the sun.

EDDIE (*peeping in*). Are yeh right Richie, come on. This warden is givin' me the evil eye out here.

RICHIE. Yeah, right Eddie. (*He gathers his things.*)

EDDIE. Alright Oweney?

OWENEY. Why wouldn't I be?

EDDIE. Oh I don't know. I just thought you might be a bit sore down around the auld solar plexus or somethin', no?

OWENEY. I'm not that fuckin' soft or anythin'.

EDDIE. Oon Oweney me boy! No hard feelings then?

OWENEY. Well let's put it this way Eddie if I was you I'd be inclined to shave meself in future.

EDDIE *chuckles.*

EDDIE. What would you say Richie?

RICHIE. I'll say nothin' till I'm there and back I think.

EDDIE. Fair play to yeh Richie. Although the way my auld jalopy is goin' lately we'll be lucky to get out of the street.

RICHIE. Why, is she actin' up on yeh?

EDDIE. A little bit, yeah. We'll be alright though. You'll have to hold the door shut mind yeh Richie. It's inclined to open of its own accord, like yeh know. I picked up this fella hitchhikin' the other day there and he fell out on me. That's a fact boy. One minute he was there, the next he was gone. Bum . . . I drove off and left him there. I didn't want him claimin' against me or anythin'. He was alright though. I could see him through the rear-view mirror, brushin' himself down and that. Can't seem to get an auld smirk out of this fella at all today Richie.

RICHIE. Yeah well Eddie . . . I mean . . . Yeh know?

EDDIE. Huh? . . . Look I'll tell yeh what I'll do, right . . .

SALLY *enters and parks her bike in the hall. EDDIE gives a little whistle and reaches out and touches her behind, much to her chagrin. She slaps him and, with a face of vengeance, slips up to LEONARD's room. EDDIE laughs.*

I'll tell yeh what I'll do. I'll let yeh hit me your best shot in the guts now. Right? Go ahead. Hit me your best.

OWENEY. Don't tempt me Eddie.

EDDIE. Hah? . . . Go ahead . . . No?

OWENEY. He probably has a galvanised vest on him or somethin'.

EDDIE. No? . . . I gave him a chance Richie. I gave yeh your chance.

OWENEY. Yeah, right.

RICHIE. I'll see yeh later on Oweney, eh?

OWENEY. Yeah, right Richie. Tell Cissy I was askin' for her.

RICHIE. Alright. (*He exits to the hall.*)

EDDIE. I got yeh two hundred smackers for fuck's sake!

Silence. EDDIE leaves. Lights rise on the hall.

Make sure you button up Richie 'cause it's freezin' cold out there. I got me aunty Cissy a nice bunch of flowers. Cheer her up a bit. I'm over here. Do yeh know how much a fella offered me for that car the other day Richie. Four hundred and fifty quid! Can yeh believe that? I mean it's an insult! Actually I only paid three hundred for it meself but that's beside the point.

EDDIE and RICHIE exit. OWENEY sighs, puts on his glasses and sits on the bench to read the morning paper. Lights down. Lights rise on LEONARD's room where MATT is working behind his easel while SALLY makes up the bed and tidies up the place etc. The fire is lighting in the grate now.

SALLY. But sure when Adam and Eve were banished from the garden, the sun and the stars and all the planets all cried for them yeh know. All except the moon who laughed. 'Cause the moon knew yeh see. That's what you should paint now. Somethin' like that. You could use real people's faces – meself and Leonard and Oweney and all. I could be the

Virgin Mary and Leonard could be one of the three Wise
Men or somethin' . . . What are yeh smirkin' at?

MATT. Nothin'.

SALLY. What? . . . (*She goes to fix up the Christmas tree.*)
Come over here and give us a hand with this thing for a
minute will yeh.

MATT. I'm tryin' to finish off a bit of work here.

SALLY. Never mind the work and come over here and help
me. I'm wantin' to fix this place up nice for Leonard before
he gets back. Hold that tree. (MATT *reluctantly goes to
her.*) Steady now . . . That's it. . . . You need to get away
from that painting for a while anyway 'cause you're just not
gettin' it if you ask me.

MATT. What's that supposed to mean?

SALLY. It means you're not gettin' it – 'cause you don't
understand it . . . You can let that go now and plug in those
lights behind yeh there.

MATT. What?

SALLY. Behind yeh. That's it. Now you're learnin'. Leonard's
eyes are much sadder than that and you gave him a cruel
mouth. Leonard doesn't have a cruel mouth. Leonard doesn't
have a cruel bone in his body . . . (*The tree lights up.*) . . .
Illumination! Deadly!

MATT. I painted what I saw.

SALLY. Yeah, an abandoned urchin with no one belongin' to
him and you gave him an auld sour mouth like your own
and somebody else's eyes. Of course I know why you done
that. Because that's the way you'd be if you were in his shoes.
But you forget that you're not him and he'll never be you.
Hang that up there will yeh (*decorations*). . . . Droop it.

MATT. Huh?

SALLY. Sort of arch it like . . . That's it. Let me see. Mmn . . .
(*She goes around the room lighting candles and Christmas
pumpkins etc.*) . . . What are yeh so sour all the time for
anyway? I mean you were reared in the lap of luxury.

MATT. The lap of luxury!

SALLY. I know where you live Matt.

MATT. I live here.

SALLY. Yeah, right.

MATT. I wouldn't expect you to understand.

SALLY. What?

MATT. The depths that some of us have to go to every day –
every minute of every day.

SALLY. Yeah, I read that book too Matt. The Agony And The
Ecstasy by Van Gogh Murphy! Here hold the other end of
that there will yeh (*a Christmas banner*). Leonard'll be
delighted when he sees this . . . Yeh see the problem with
you Matt is you don't know how to love and you'll never be
a good artist until you do.

MATT. I know how to love. I've been in love.

SALLY. Yeah with who though? (*She looks into the mirror and
primps.*) . . . Of course like most men you probably think
that you have a divine right to be loved or somethin' do
yeh? Well I'm here to tell yeh that yeh haven't. Nobody
has. I mean you have to be able to recognise love when it
comes along Matt otherwise it'll go away again on yeh.
Your problem is you're not able to recognise it. Or maybe
you don't want to of course. And there should be no limits
to lovin' someone either. Yeh know? Nothin' yeh wouldn't
do, nowhere you wouldn't go. I mean how can you even
hope to be a real artist without a muse, Matt? And how can
yeh find a muse if you don't know how to love her? Huh?

MATT. Thanks for the life lesson and all but . . . (*He indicates
his work.*)

SALLY. Yeah . . . Well . . . Don't forget to change those eyes
and that mouth. Otherwise you might as well paint a picture
of yourself and be done with it.

MATT *indignantly takes the painting from the easel and
storms out the door.*

SALLY (*calling after him*). Oh and Leonard doesn't have big ears either. I mean he's not Labhraic Loinseach or anythin' yeh know!

MATT crosses the landing to his own room. SALLY takes a rug from her bag and spreads it out in front of the fire. She takes a look around at the room and smiles at its cosiness. Lights down. Lights rise on the hall where MAEVE is on the telephone.

MAEVE. Hello P.J. It's Maeve. When yeh get this message yeh might come round to the shop will yeh. All the lights are out and the phone is dead and everything. The place is in darkness over there. On Christmas Eve! I mean what's goin' on? If you know what's goin' on come round and tell me will yeh and not have me whatdoyoucallit . . . If you don't know what's goin' on come round anyway 'cause I don't know what to do about it. I mean I've a load of people comin' to look at stuff today. Anyway come round as soon as yeh can. Sooner!

OWENEY is standing in the doorway of the shop, watching her. SALLY crosses the landing with the easel, raps on MATT's door and leans the easel against the wall.

SALLY (*to OWENEY below*). Some friend you turned out to be. You get the Christmas tree and he takes the blame. Nice one! . . . I'm queer disappointed in you boy!

She goes back inside the bedsit.

MAEVE. Was your electricity off at any stage Oweney?

OWENEY. No.

MAEVE. Mine is. The phone is gone dead too. The place is in darkness over there – on Christmas Eve! I mean what's goin' on?

OWENEY. Is your till workin'?

MAEVE. No. Nothin's workin'. My tree and everything is dead. It's dismal lookin' over there so it is. I wouldn't mind but I had it lookin' really nice.

OWENEY. Do yeh want me to come over and check the fuse box for yeh?

MAEVE. It's not a fuse Oweney. Somethin's up and I don't know what. I'm goin' to tell yeh one thing if P.J. cut me off I'll strangle him. I mean it's Christmas Eve like. I don't know. I've a load of people comin' to look at stuff today too. Tch . . . Every time I try to do somethin'. I mean he was the very same with the gallery that time. Mind you I suppose I should have recognised the danger in the first place anyway. 'Cause he never had anything to really say for himself – except about things. His things!

OWENEY. Listen, come on, I'll make yeh a quick cup of coffee – calm yeh down a bit.

MAEVE. No, I can't. I left the door ajar over there. I'd better get back before the place is rifled on me.

OWENEY. Well hang on a minute then, I've somethin' for yeh.

MAEVE. Huh?

OWENEY *goes into the shop.* SALLY *comes out onto the landing with a Christmas pumpkin. She lays it down and proceeds to light a candle inside it.*

SALLY. What's up with you?

MAEVE. I don't know. I've been hung out to dry I think.

SALLY. That figures.

MAEVE. Huh?

OWENEY *returns with a little wrapped-up present.* SALLY *throws him a dirty look as she exits.*

OWENEY. Happy Christmas. In case I don't see yeh.

MAEVE. What? . . . Oweney! Thanks . . . Jesus . . . Can I open it now?

OWENEY. If yeh want.

MAEVE. I know I'm bold and all but I will. Cheer me up a bit. (*She opens it up to reveal a pair of gloves.*) . . . Just what I need, hah?

OWENEY. They came in three sizes – big, small and dainty.
Needless to say I picked the dainty 'cause . . . that's the
kind of man I am.

MAEVE. Dainty is a bit big for me actually. No smaller, no?
Where did yeh buy these by the way?

OWENEY. Anna's.

MAEVE. Anna's Boutique?

OWENEY. Anna's! It never said nothin' about boutique. Over
the door anyway.

She throws him a dirty look.

MAEVE. What's the place like?

OWENEY. It's a dump. You'll never catch me in there again
anyway. And if I was you I'd wear those gloves under
protest. Cut the labels off and all.

MAEVE. It's alright, I'll use them to strangle P.J. with when
I find him.

OWENEY. Yeah well whatever yeh do don't leave them behind
yeh at the scene of the crime will yeh 'cause the trail leads
right back to me yeh know. Oweney Clark, you are charged
with the murder of P.J. Dawson because they say you are in
love with his wife. How do yeh plead? Guilty your honour.
Of murder? No your honour, of loving his wife!

Pause as she softens towards him.

MAEVE. No one ever gives me presents. Thanks Oweney.
They're deadly and soft!

She kisses him.

OWENEY. Mmn . . .

Pause.

MAEVE. Candles.

OWENEY. Huh?

MAEVE. Loads of candles all over the place. See yeh Oweney.
(*She kisses him again and quickly leaves.*) . . . Thanks for
the gloves.

OWENEY. Yeah . . . Thanks for the kiss.

He watches her go, turning to see MATT *gazing down at him from the landing.* MATT *takes the easel and goes back inside. Lights down. Lights rise on the barbershop. It is late afternoon. Darkness is beginning to invade the room.* OWENEY *sets up a little foldaway table in front of the bench – tablecloth, basket of food, glass of wine etc.* MAEVE's *voice can be heard coming from the living quarters.*

MAEVE. This kettle is boilin' here Oweney. Do yeh want me to make the tea or what?

OWENEY. No, I'll do that. Come out here and eat this while it's hot.

MAEVE *enters.*

MAEVE. Aw Oweney, that's lovely. A glass of wine and all.

OWENEY. Sit down there.

MAEVE. What is that – bruschetta? (*She sits and eats.*)

OWENEY. Yeah. There's some toasted sandwiches there too – cheese and ham and tomato. Heat yeh up a bit. I'd say it was fairly cold over there today was it?

MAEVE. Freezing. Are you not havin' anything, no?

OWENEY. No. I had somethin' earlier on. Are yeh wantin' tea or coffee?

MAEVE. Tea please.

OWENEY *has gone down to the living quarters.*

This is lovely Oweney. Thanks.

OWENEY (*off*). Huh?

MAEVE. Oh I didn't tell yeh did I? I found the little wood after.

OWENEY (*off*). Yeah. Got there without me, hah?

MAEVE. Yeah. And you're right, it is lovely. With the little river running through it! Strange place though. Kind of weird yeh know. The trees sort of talkin' to each other and all. (*She gives a little shudder.*) . . . To tell yeh the truth I was half expectin' to meet myself there at one stage. My face in the water or somethin'. Or camped beside the river. Only younger though yeh know. More whatdoyoucallit . . . I don't know . . . defiant or somethin' . . . When I got back to the shop that day I had to sign for a parcel and I instinctively found myself scribbling out my maiden name. Don't ask me why. I haven't done that in years. Maeve O'Connor – the girl I used to be! (OWENEY *enters with a pot of tea.*) . . . You'd like to meet her wouldn't yeh?

OWENEY. Who's that?

MAEVE. The girl I use to be!

OWENEY (*doubling back for a table mat*). Huh? . . . I thought I had.

She shakes her head emphatically. He reaches out and plucks a crumb from her lips and eats it. She smiles, flattered. OWENEY sits and basks in her radiance.

MAEVE (*taking his hand*). Oh Oweney, it's not fair. We could have so much fun together – you and me. Going places and all. You'd take me places wouldn't yeh?

OWENEY. Oh yeah.

MAEVE. Where would yeh take me?

OWENEY. Don't know. I'd take yeh to the pictures. Take yeh to the pub. I might take yeh dancin' now and then.

MAEVE. Would yeh take me out to lunch?

OWENEY. Take yeh out to lunch.

MAEVE. We could go to recitals too couldn't we? During the festival!

OWENEY. I don't see why not.

MAEVE. We might even go to the opera sometime, hah!

OWENEY. Oh here now I'm not feckin' made of money or anythin'.

She laughs.

MAEVE. This is one of the loveliest things anyone ever done for me yeh know.

OWENEY. Yeah?

MAEVE. Yeah.

She runs her fingers through his hair. A beautiful moment. The phone rings and, eventually, OWENEY *reluctantly lets go her hand, rises and goes out to the hall to answer it.*

OWENEY (*as he goes*). The girl yeh used to be hah!

MAEVE (*calling out to him*). Mmn . . . That's what my mother said to me the morning I was leaving the house to get married Oweney yeh know.

OWENEY. Yeh what? . . . Hello . . . Yeah, speaking. No, he's not here at the moment. Who's calling please?

MAEVE. Never mind who you were or who you are she said and . . .

OWENEY (*off*). Oh right. Yeah . . . When did this happen? Oh right. Sorry to hear that now . . .

MAEVE. . . . just try and concentrate on who you're supposed to be.

OWENEY. Yeah I'll tell him when he gets here. I say I'll tell him. Yeah. O.K.

MAEVE. Sound advice really when yeh think of it. I suppose. I mean then all I had to do was try and figure out who I'm supposed to be . . .

OWENEY (*off*). Thanks for calling . . . Yeah. Bye.

OWENEY *returns to the shop.*

MAEVE. . . . and . . . just whatdoyoucallit . . . I don't know . . . pretend to be it . . . What's up?

OWENEY. Richie's wife . . . She's gone.

Lights down. Lights rise on the shop. RICHIE *is sitting by the window.* EDDIE *is standing beside the sink.* MAEVE *enters.*

MAEVE. Richie. Are yeh alright? What happened? (*She goes to him.*)

RICHIE. I don't know to tell yeh the truth. She was grand before we left. We must have been only gone a few miles down the road when Oweney got a call here to say she had just passed away in her sleep. But sure by then we were nearly halfway home, like yeh know. Poor Oweney had to give me the bad news when I arrived here.

MAEVE. And are yeh alright for a lift back up there and all?

RICHIE. I think so. We're alright Eddie ain't we?

EDDIE. Yeah, I'm goin' to borrow me da's car. We're just waitin' on me mother now. She's gone over to see the undertaker and all the rest of it. To be honest with yeh Richie I'd be afraid to take my auld banger in case it let us down or anything, yeh know.

RICHIE. Yeah?

MAEVE. But sure I'll drop yeh up that far if yeh like Richie. And I'm not just sayin' that now.

RICHIE. Oh I know that missus. Thanks all the same.

MAEVE. Huh? . . . His hands are freezin'.

LEONARD *pops his head in the door.*

LEONARD. Is Oweney around?

EDDIE. He'll be back in a minute. He just popped over to the bettin' shop. How did you get on after?

LEONARD. Alright. Thirty pounds. And another thirty for the solicitor. (*He shrugs.*)

EDDIE. That's not bad. Are yeh only out of it now?

LEONARD. I was the last to be called. (*He shrugs it off like a delinquent.*)

EDDIE. What did the judge say to yeh?

LEONARD. Oh he thought it was very funny. Made a bit of a skit of me to tell yeh the truth.

EDDIE. The Christmas spirit I suppose. A couple of glasses of port in him or somethin'.

LEONARD. I don't know about that. He gave big Hank Thomas nine months sure.

EDDIE. Oh that's right big Hank was up today wasn't he? Nine months! Jaysus that's stiff!

MAEVE. Hank? He works for P.J. don't he?

EDDIE. Yeah, he does the odd auld job for him alright. From time to time like.

MAEVE. What was he up for?

EDDIE. I don't know that.

LEONARD. He broke a fella's nose outside the Banjo Bar one night. P.J. was up in the court actually – standin' down the back.

MAEVE. Was he?

LEONARD. I'm goin' to tell yeh one thing but it was like the Wild West up there at one stage. Hank was up for breakin' your man's nose, there was another lad up for hittin' a fella in the forehead with a hatchet and Malachy Morris was charged with knockin' off a horse and cart.

EDDIE. Oh I heard about that alright. Malachy was like Lash Larue comin' down the street I believe with the squad car after him – sirens goin' and everything. (*He yelps and cracks an imaginary whip.*) Don't tell me – bound to the peace and he's not even to look at another horse, right?

Laughter. Awkward silence.

MAEVE. Give us a shout if yeh need anything Richie.

RICHIE. Right missus. Thanks.

She moves to the door.

MAEVE. Can't seem to get her face out of my head Richie!

RICHIE. Makes two of us.

Pause.

MAEVE. See yeh lads.

EDDIE. All the best.

LEONARD. Bye.

MAEVE. Look after him now, do yeh hear me.

EDDIE. That'll be alright. (*She leaves.*) . . . There was no names or anything mentioned up there today I hope was there?

LEONARD. Names? No. I never said nothin' anyway.

EDDIE. Good. Happy Christmas so

LEONARD. What? (EDDIE *gives him the bend to go.*) . . . Oh yeah, right . . .

> LEONARD *leaves, glancing joyfully at* SALLY*'s bike in the hall. He hurries up the stairs and into his own room.*

EDDIE. Scarface, hah!

RICHIE. What's that?

EDDIE. Your man.

RICHIE. What about him?

EDDIE. I say he was up in court today.

RICHIE. Oh yeah . . . How did he get on I wonder?

EDDIE. Thirty pounds he says and another thirty for the solicitor.

RICHIE. Yeah? . . . Dear enough too!

EDDIE. Mmn . . .

> LEONARD *is disappointed to find the room empty. He comes out onto the landing as* OWENEY *comes through the front door.*

OWENEY. Leonard! How did yeh get on?

LEONARD. Thirty pounds. And thirty for the solicitor. (*He shrugs.*)

OWENEY. A dear lift home in other words Leonard, hah!

LEONARD. Mmn – surely was.

OWENEY. Ah well. Oh listen I think I got yeh a job.

LEONARD. Yeah?

OWENEY. Yeah, the Town Clerk was here this mornin' for a shave and he said there's a caretakin' job goin' above in the new Municipal Buildin'. You're to go up and see him after Christmas.

LEONARD. Yeah? And what are the chances would yeh say?

OWENEY. Fairly good I'd say. But sure he knows your form anyway.

LEONARD. Let's hope this thing don't go in the paper though Oweney.

OWENEY. Leonard, yeh knocked off a few Christmas trees. I mean you're not Jesse James or anything.

LEONARD. All the same.

EDDIE (*enters*). I'm goin' over to get the car Oweney.

OWENEY. Yeah right. Sixty pounds it cost him.

EDDIE. So I heard.

OWENEY. Never mind Leonard, meself and the queer fella here'll chip in a few quid towards it. (EDDIE *throws him a dirty look.*) . . . Come on now Eddie and have a heart. He kept his mouth shut didn't he?

EDDIE. Oweney, I've enough on me plate now with me aunty Cissy dyin' without havin' to worry about that fella. I mean Jesus, yeh know . . . I'm in mournin' here. Hank Thomas got nine months too he was tellin' me.

OWENEY. Good. I hope he gets a knife up his hole and he in there.

EDDIE. Hey.

OWENEY. Fuckin' bully boy goin' around!

EDDIE. I'll have you know mate that he's a colleague of mine, yeh know.

OWENEY. We'll see how brave he is now then. Where are they sendin' him anyway – Mountjoy?

LEONARD. I don't know that.

EDDIE. Yes, a dear and trusted colleague at that!

OWENEY *throws him a dirty look.*

LEONARD. Have yeh any idea where Sally is, Oweney?

OWENEY. She's in Matt's room there. He said no one was to disturb them.

LEONARD. Oh, right.

EDDIE. I told yeh not to turn your back on her didn't I – that she'd let yeh down. What did I say to yeh? Hah? . . . Keep an eye on Richie for me there Oweney will yeh.

OWENEY. Yeah, right. Is he alright?

EDDIE. Yeah. (*He makes a dubious sign.*) . . . I'll give him a bamp. Listen out for me will yeh.

EDDIE *exits.*

OWENEY. Yeah, right.

LEONARD. I thought Matt was supposed to be goin' out home today.

Pause. SALLY*'s laughter can be heard coming from* MATT*'s room.* OWENEY *goes into the barbershop.* LEONARD *comes sadly down the stairs towards the telephone. Lights rise on the barbershop.*

OWENEY. Alright Richie?

RICHIE. Yeah. Eddie's just gone to get the car and that. Oh whatshername from across the street was here too while you were out.

OWENEY. Who's that? Maeve?

RICHIE. Yeah. She just came over to sympathise and that.

OWENEY. Oh, right. That was nice of her. She's like Madame Houdini over there with all the candles. She's just gone is she?

RICHIE. Yeah, yeh just missed her.

OWENEY. She's in the dark over there.

RICHIE. Aye?

OWENEY. Mmn . . . Well I'm after winnin' a nice handy little
two hundred smackers for meself anyway Richie . . .
Twenty pound win double on Sergeant Major and Planxty
Jones. 3 to 1 and 5 to 4 . . . (*He puts the money in the
cashbox.*) . . . So don't be stuck Richie, right.

RICHIE. What's that? . . . Oh, right Oweney. Thanks.

OWENEY (*sings softly*).
Take My Love Take This Crochet Di Oro
It Will Bring You Home Safely To Me . . .

Lights down. Lights rise on the hall where LEONARD *is on
the telephone.*

LEONARD. Hello. Could I speak to Bernadette please.
Bernadette Carroll. Yeah. Please . . . Tell her it's her brother
Leonard. Thanks . . . Hello Bernadette. How are yeh? It's
Leonard. Yeah. Just ringin' to wish yeh a Happy Christmas.
Yeah, the same to you Bernadette. How are yeh gettin' on?
That's good. The job is goin' alright, yeah? That's good.
And what about Tommy? He's in the pub already? He's
startin' early, hah! Yeah. Did yeh get my card alright? Yeah.
Ah not at all. Sure it's only a few shillin's Bernadette . . .
No, nothin' doin' yet Bernadette. Yeah, I've been lookin'
around yeh know but so far there's nothin' doin'. I've an
interview with the Town Clerk after Christmas. The new
Municipal buildin' or somethin'. Ah I'll find somethin'
alright. A man of my calibre! I don't know about now.

SALLY *comes out onto the landing,* MATT *at her heels.*

SALLY. Leonard. How did yeh get on?

LEONARD (*cupping the phone*). Thirty pounds and another
thirty for the solicitor. A dear lift home in other words.

SALLY. Mmn . . . Matt took one look at me and he said he just
had to draw me. Didn't yeh? He said I had a certain lunar

majesty. I don't know whether that's a good thing or not.
Who are yeh talkin' to?

LEONARD. Me sister Bernadette.

SALLY. Yeah? In England?

LEONARD. Mmn . . . No, I'm talkin' to Sally, Bernadette. Me
girlfriend. Yeah, me first.

SALLY (*shouting*). And his last Bernadette.

LEONARD. She said and me last. Yeah. She is. She said yeh
sound mad.

SALLY. Lunar majesty.

LEONARD. She said it's lunar majesty . . . No, lunar . . . Yeah.

SALLY. Tell her I was askin' for her.

LEONARD. Yeah, right . . . Alright Bernadette. Have a lovely
Christmas and I'll probably talk to you again in the New
Year sometime. Wish Tommy the best for me. Yeah, right.
Bye Bernadette. Bye . . . She's gone.

He hangs up and goes up the stairs.

SALLY (*taking his hand*). Come on, I'll show yeh the picture.

LEONARD. I thought Matt was supposed to be superstitious
about that?

SALLY. It's Christmas. That right Matt?

MATT. What?

SALLY. Did yeh see the room?

LEONARD. Yeah.

SALLY. What did yeh think? Deadly ain't it?

LEONARD. Not without you in it, no!

SALLY. Aw! . . . I'm goin' to get him to change that picture of
you too. Did yeh see the big ears he gave yeh? Labhraig
Loinseach!

LEONARD. Oweney thinks he got me a job Sally. He said the
Town Clerk was in this mornin' for a shave and . . .

The are gone inside. Lights rise on the shop. OWENEY is by the window now.

OWENEY. Did she say anything before she went Richie?

RICHIE. No. Not while I was there anyway. The nurse said she thought she called my name at one stage but she couldn't be sure. I'd like to think she did mind yeh – after all we've been through like!

OWENEY. Huh?

A car horn bamps. RICHIE rises and fastens his coat etc. Lights down on the shop. Lights rise on the hall. MATT is standing on the landing, smoking a cigarette. RICHIE comes out of the shop. He stops in the hall to gaze up into MATT's vacant eyes. RICHIE exits. MATT stubs out his cigarette.

MATT. Leonard, come out here will yeh and give us a hand with somethin'.

LEONARD (*enters*). What's that?

MATT. Take these down to the street for me Leonard will yeh?

MATT disappears inside and emerges with cans of paint, brushes, a floor cloth and canvas etc. SALLY is at his heels.

LEONARD. What for?

MATT. I'm goin' to paint that auld hoarding.

LEONARD. The hotel hoarding?

MATT. Yeah. It'll be my present to the people. They'll wake up in the mornin' and there it'll be – starin' them in the face. And then they'll never forget this Christmas day.

SALLY. Yes!

LEONARD. What about P.J?

MATT. What about him?

LEONARD. Do yeh think you should ask him like?

MATT. What for?

LEONARD. Well it is his hotel Matt.

SALLY. Do yeh want me to carry somethin', Matt?

MATT. Yeah, see if you can manage that little stepladder in there will yeh?

SALLY. Right. What are yeh goin' to draw Matt?

MATT. You'll see.

SALLY. Alright. People of this place – I love you!

They trample down the stairs. Lights down. Lights rise on the barbershop. OWENEY *is having a cup of tea while a paint-splattered* MATT *hangs around, lighting up a cigarette.* LEONARD *enters, looking busy.*

LEONARD. There's a fair crowd gathered around there now Matt. Your man Harney is startin' up on the auld guitar and everything. (*He sings.*) And So This Is – Christmas.

OWENEY. That's one way of bringin' it to P.J.'s attention I suppose.

LEONARD. Power to the people Oweney.

OWENEY. Che Guevara where he is!

LEONARD. Yeh might plug in that behind yeh there Oweney will yeh (*an extension lead*). . . . till we try to give this man a bit of light out there. It's lookin' fairly good Matt. Did yeh see it Oweney?

OWENEY. Mmn.

LEONARD. It's good ain't it? The moon grinnin' at the two of them in the background though, hah! That's it now I'd say Matt.

MATT. Yeah?

OWENEY. All I can say is that the two of you are queer lucky big Hank Thomas is in Mountjoy or he'd've been down here to wrap that step ladder around one of your necks by now.

SALLY (*from the landing*). Leonard. Your tea is ready.

LEONARD (*going out to the hall*). What's that?

SALLY. I say your tea is ready.

LEONARD. Oh yeah, right.

SALLY. Is Matt wantin' to join us for tea or what?

LEONARD. I don't know that . . . Matt are you wantin' to join us for tea or what?

MATT. No. I've to get back to work – try and finish this thing.

LEONARD. No, he's not.

SALLY. Is he wantin' a sambo?

LEONARD. Are yeh wantin' a sambo Matt?

MATT. I don't know. What's in them?

LEONARD. He wants to know what's in them?

SALLY. Sheep's thing and onion . . . What's in them! (*She goes into the room.*)

LEONARD. Sheep's thing and onion she says.

MATT. What?

LEONARD. Cheese and ham and lettuce and tomato and all I suppose.

MATT. Huh? . . . Alright, go on then, I'll chance one.

LEONARD. Yeah? Risk it for a biscuit. Are you wantin' one Oweney?

OWENEY. No thanks. (LEONARD *hurries up the stairs.*) Oh Leonard!

LEONARD (*from the landing*). Yeah?

OWENEY. How far would you be only I called yeh?

LEONARD. Oweney!

OWENEY. Leonard! . . . He's in his alley.

LEONARD *titters as he goes into the room where* SALLY *has the table set for tea.* MAEVE *is standing by the window.*

LEONARD. He says he'll chance one.

SALLY. That's nice of him. Give us a kiss.

LEONARD. What? . . . Oh yeah, right. (*They kiss.*)

SALLY. Don't ever come into a room or go out of it without kissin' me, right.

LEONARD. O.K. So much to remember though, yeh know.

SALLY. Yeah well, don't forget.

LEONARD. Nothin' stirrin' out there yet, no?

MAEVE. No.

LEONARD. But sure I don't suppose she'll be buried till the day after Steven's Day now will she?

MAEVE. Huh?

SALLY. Look forget about all that will yeh and take this down to him. Life is for livin'. Is Oweney wantin' one?

LEONARD. No.

SALLY. Here take him one anyway. Go ahead. And don't be there till you're back.

LEONARD. Right . . . Oh! (*He doubles back to kiss her.*)

SALLY. You're learnin'.

LEONARD *exits.* SALLY *chuckles and makes a pot of tea.*

SALLY. Yes – life is for livin'! Amn't I right?

MAEVE. Huh? . . . Mmn . . . I was just thinking about the last time I went up to the nursing home to see her – poor Richie fussing with the flowers at the foot of the bed as she lay there with her face to the wall. And later on I held her hand and she confided in me. It'd been years since she laughed out loud she said and she could hardly remember the last time she cried. Learnt nothing worth talkin' about along the way either as far as I could see – except how to hurt and be hurt! Although she ran away on him and everything one time she was telling me. Lived in a basement flat in Swansea or somewhere for a couple of months. Got a job in a little book shop over there, reverted to her own name again, walked through the park in the rain and all the rest of it. But of course he eventually followed her and found her and brought her home again. Not that he didn't love or anything. I'm sure he did but . . . Sometimes that's not enough yeh know . . . Here she comes. I'll slip over to the chapel I think. Poor Richie looks broken-hearted. The funeral, Leonard.

LEONARD (*returning*). Huh?

MAEVE. I hope they won't get a fright when they turn the corner. That mural wasn't even there this evenin' when they left.

LEONARD enters as MAEVE leaves. OWENEY is waiting for her at the foot of the stairs, munching a sandwich. They exit together. LEONARD and SALLY kiss.

SALLY. How can love not be enough?

LEONARD. What?

They sit at the table and have their tea. Lights down. Lights rise on the bedsit. LEONARD is asleep on the bed. A sing-song can be heard coming from the shop below. LEONARD wakes and looks around him. Lights rise on the shop. OWENEY, RICHIE, EDDIE, MAEVE and SALLY are singing, OWENEY leading the song. MATT is at the window.

We Are Poor Little Lambs Who Have Lost Our Way
Ba Ba Ba
Little Black Sheep Who Have Gone Astray
Ba Ba Ba.

OWENEY (*solo*).
Gentlemen, Songsters Out On A Spree
Doomed From Here To Eternity
May The Lord Have Mercy On Such As We
Ba Ba Ba.

LEONARD. Sally . . . Sally.

LEONARD rises and goes searching for SALLY, rapping on MATT's door and peeping inside etc, and finally coming down the stairs to the party-cum-wake.

ALL (*in harmony*).
  We Are Poor Little Lambs
  Who Have Lost Our Way
  Ba Ba Ba
  Little Black Sheep
  Who Have Gone Astray
  Ba Ba Ba.

  Applause etc as LEONARD *enters. What follows is a*
  beautiful cacophony of interweaving and overlapping
  voices.

SALLY (*taking* LEONARD*'s hand*). Here he is now – sleepy
  head.

LEONARD. What?

MAEVE. That's a lovely song Oweney.

LEONARD. Where did yeh go? I was lookin' all over the place
  for yeh.

OWENEY. What? Yeah. The Whiffinpoof Song!

SALLY. I went up to midnight mass.

MAEVE. It's a lovely song Richie ain't it?

RICHIE. Yeah. The Whiffinpoof Song. Yeah!

SALLY. You were dead to the world sure . . . The big sleepy
  head on yeh!

LEONARD. Yeh what? I was lookin' all over the place for yeh.

SALLY. Yeah well, now yeh found me!

EDDIE (*sings*)
  There's A Table Down at Murrays.
  There's A Spot Where Louis Dwells.

MATT. There's someone out there Oweney – standing in the
  shadows across the street there.

OWENEY. What? Yeah! . . . What are yeh drinkin' Leonard?

LEONARD. I don't know Oweney. What have yeh got?

MAEVE. 'From Here to Eternity.' I wonder is that where it comes from?

RICHIE. What's that?

OWENEY. I have whiskey, vodka, stout, beer and a little bottle of champagne – thanks to Maeve.

MAEVE. I say 'From Here to Eternity.' I wonder is that where they got it like?

RICHIE. I don't know that now. Probably. What? The film yeh mean?

MAEVE. Mmn.

EDDIE (*sings*).
   There's A One Eyed Yellow Idol
   Just North Of Kathmandu . . . (*He laughs.*)

LEONARD. I don't normally but I'll have a little glass of champagne because of the night that's in it.

OWENEY. Oon Leonard me boy!

MAEVE (*tidying up*). It's a very unusual song.

EDDIE. That song was written about a crowd of soldiers who were about to go on a dangerous mission from which they would never return.

LEONARD. I'll probably fall up the stairs mind yeh – after this.

OWENEY. Not at all.

SALLY. But sure that's my third one Leonard. (*She giggles.*)

EDDIE. And what's more they all knew it too. Hence the line: 'Doomed From Here To Eternity.' And yes, in answer to your question, you're right, that is where it comes from . . . 'From Here to Eternity.' Montgomery Clift. 'I just saw it in a shop and bought it.' (*He fiddles with his tie.*) Or was that 'The Young Lions'?

MATT. I'm off Oweney.

OWENEY. What's that?

MATT. I say here's me lift. (*He gathers his things.*)

OWENEY. Oh yeah, right Matt.

MAEVE (*from the living room*). You've no milk Oweney.

OWENEY. Why, is someone wantin' tea or somethin'?

EDDIE (*sings*).
There's A Table Down At Murray's . . .

No wait there now . . .

MAEVE. No, for yourself for the mornin' I mean.

EDDIE. Somethin' a little more whatdoyoucallit I think . . .

OWENEY. Oh right. Hang on Matt and I'll let yeh out.

RICHIE. But sure I've lashin's of milk over there Oweney. I'll leave a carton outside your door in the mornin' on my way to mass if yeh like.

EDDIE. Hang on now . . .

OWENEY *goes out to the hall.*

OWENEY. Good man Richie . . .

EDDIE (*sings*).
Many A Tear Has To Fall . . .

SALLY (*to* MAEVE). Here you, how can love not be enough?

MAEVE. Yeh what?

OWENEY. I'm not lookin' to get rid of yeh or anythin' Matt. I just want to make sure that no one else gets in.

EDDIE (*sings*).
But It's All In The Game

Some of the others join in

All In the Wonderful Game That We Know As Love . . .

OWENEY (*opening the front door and looking up and down the street*). Little Tommy Day and the boys are on the rampage, like yeh know.

MATT. Yeah?

OWENEY. Have a good day tomorrow.

MATT. You too Oweney. What are yeh goin' to do anyway?

OWENEY. Meself and Leonard are goin' down as far as The Whole Hog for our dinner – twenty quid for the lot. Turkey and ham and everything man! Sure where would yeh be goin', hah?

MATT. That's what I say. See yeh Oweney . . . Happy Christmas.

OWENEY. Yeah right Matt. The same to you. See yeh Steven's Day or whenever, eh?

MATT *exits as* MAEVE *comes out, closing the door to the shop, shutting out the sound of the singing inside.*

MAEVE. I'm goin' to go too Oweney. Is everyone alright for a lift and all, yeah?

OWENEY. Yeah, they're alright Maeve. Get out of here while you're ahead if I was you. Did P.J. see the whatdoyoucallit yet? (*The hoarding.*)

MAEVE. No, not yet.

OWENEY. No? I'd be very interested in seein' his reaction to that now.

MAEVE. Mmn. Can't wait.

OWENEY. Who do Adam and Eve remind yeh of?

MAEVE. What? . . . Oh my God! . . . I'll kill him.

OWENEY. That little startled look.

MAEVE. I hate that look . . . I'll kill him. I mean if P.J. twigs that like! I wouldn't mind but he made you real good lookin' in it.

OWENEY. I'm better lookin' than that.

MAEVE. What, in reality yeh mean? . . . He's dead! . . . I got yeh a present. (*She indicates a wrapped-up present leaning against the wall.*) . . . Not to be opened under any circumstances until the morning.

OWENEY. I let you open yours.

MAEVE. I knew you'd say that. Here, you can open this little one (*a small present*).

OWENEY. Yeah? . . . Deadly! Nothin' for the rest of them, no? (*She hushes him up.*) Thanks very much. (*He opens it up to find a scarf.*) Oh lovely. Anna's Boutique or did yeh knit it yourself?

MAEVE. Yeah, two plain and one purl – or somethin'.

OWENEY (*wrapping the scarf around him like a college boy*). I say dear boy! . . . Where' your gloves?

MAEVE. I have them here – me dainty gloves.

OWENEY. Well put them on yeh. That's it. Now we're right for the winter. I've the scarf and you've the gloves . . . Sort of sums us up really don't it?

They chuckle.

Have you no scarf?

She shakes her head like a little girl.

OWENEY. Well here you can have a loan of mine. And don't forget where you got it. (*He wraps it around her.*) Where's your hat?

MAEVE. Me pocket.

He takes her hat from her pocket and puts it on her head.

OWENEY. It's freezin' cauld out there yeh know . . . Now you're right. (*He looks at her lovingly.*) . . . Could start a new trend yeh know.

MAEVE. Yeh reckon?

OWENEY. I do. Sure all the women were talkin' about you comin' out of the shop the other day there. Maeve said mauve to go with my hair which she says is dunduckery grey – the colour of a mouse's arse.

MAEVE (*titters*). Mrs Costello.

OWENEY. Yeah. Pink hair and an arse like an iceberg.

She laughs. He puts his arm around her and she lays her head on his shoulder and they fall silent. A little bell chimes in the distance.

OWENEY. St Mary's little bell, hah! – callin' all the orphans home. You'd be sort of tempted wouldn't yeh? (*She nods and chuckles sadly.*) . . . A real sad little clang off of it.

MAEVE (*sinking a little deeper into him*). Mmn . . .

OWENEY. Maybe we should say a little prayer or somethin' should we?

MAEVE. What for? I already got what I want.

He laughs. They kiss. Pause.

MAEVE. . . . Adam and Eve won't go down too well yeh know.

OWENEY. I know. And to make matters worse as soon as you're gone I'm goin' to carve your name in the snow. Maeve O'Connor – the girl she used to be!

MAEVE. Don't you dare.

OWENEY. No?

MAEVE. No . . . You're not to . . . If yeh do decide to do it though make sure yeh use a capital M will yeh?

OWENEY. Maeve with a capital M . . . Right.

She chuckles. They kiss. Pause.

MAEVE. Better go, eh.

OWENEY. Yeah, right Maeve . . . Have a nice day tomorrow.

MAEVE. Yeah. You too . . . (*She lets his hand go and backs away.*) . . . I like this scarf mind yeh. Sorry I gave it to yeh now . . . (*She exits, calling as she goes.*) . . . Happy Christmas Oweney.

OWENEY (*calling after her*). Happy Christmas Maeve.

He picks up the wrapped-up present in the hall, closes the front door and goes back to the shop.

ALL (*singing*).
And Your Heart Will Fly Away.

*Lights down. Lights rise. It is Christmas morning. A carton
of milk is outside the front door. OWENEY is coming out of
the living quarters in a dishevelled state. He goes out to
fetch the milk. SALLY and LEONARD come out of the
bedsit and onto the landing. They kiss. SALLY is dressed.
LEONARD is still in his pyjamas. SALLY puts on her new
hat and descends the stairs. Her bicycle is parked in the
hall. She rolls it out the door.*

OWENEY. Good man Richie (*the milk*).

SALLY. Happy Christmas Oweney.

OWENEY. Yeah right Sally – the same to you. Like the hat!

SALLY. Thanks.

She exits.

LEONARD. Alright Oweney?

OWENEY. Yeah. As long as I don't have Sister Assumta down
here after me of course. I'm goin' to do a bit of a fry-up this
mornin' Leonard. Are yeh wantin' to join me or what?

LEONARD. That'd be nice Oweney. Hang on and I'll get
dressed.

OWENEY. Please do – before yeh put me off me grapefruit!
Not that I have any grapefruit mind yeh!

*OWENEY goes inside as LEONARD slips back into the
bedsit. OWENEY turns on the radio – 'Rocking Around the
Christmas Tree' by Brenda Lee. He sits in the chair and
unwraps a few presents – a tie, a jumper, a C.D. etc. Then
he turns to MAEVE's present. It is a painting of OWENEY.
He sits dumbfounded. Lights down on the shop. Lights
rise on the bedsit where LEONARD can be seen dancing
around the room to the same tune on his radio. Lights
down. Bing Crosby sings 'White Christmas' and we hear the
sounds of The Whole Hog – men talking and joking, cutlery
clattering, delph jangling, the sound of lonely laughter.
Lights rise on the empty bedsit. The fire is lighting, the*

*Christmas tree is glowing and a sad sacred streak of
afternoon sunlight streams into the room.* OWENEY *has
left the radio on in the shop down below and we faintly hear
Bing Crosby singing 'White Christmas' from afar. Lights
down. Lights rise on the shop. It is late afternoon and the
evening shadows are beginning to fall around the room.
Elvis Presley is singing 'Crying in the Chapel' on the radio.
The painting of* OWENEY *is hanging on the wall. Lights
rise to find* RICHIE *knocking on the front door. He receives
no reply, muffles up and exits. Lights rise on the bedsit. It is
late evening.* LEONARD *and* SALLY *are in bed together,
lost in each other's arms in a classic lover's pose. A
selection box of chocolates lies open on the end of the bed.
Some modern tune can be heard coming from the radio
below in the shop. Lights down. Lights rise on the hall and
landing.* MATT *staggers in from the street, badly hurt and
bleeding. With a frightened look in his eyes he stumbles up
the stairs, falls and curls up somewhere in the shadows on
the landing. Lights down. Lights rise on the shop. The place
has been ransacked – sink torn out, chair overturned,
mirror smashed, bench ripped from the wall and newspapers
and magazines and bric-a-brac strewn all about. The living
quarters too are wrecked.* OWENEY *is sitting on the
remnants of the bench, singing into a walkie-talkie.*

OWENEY.
I Peeped In And On Her Bed
In Gay Profusion Lying There
Lovely Ribbons Scarlet Ribbons
Scarlet Ribbons For Her Hair.

MAEVE *enters from the street. She stands in the doorway,
saddened by the destruction.* OWENEY *gently urges her to
come in.*

OWENEY (*into the walkie-talkie*). I am doin' the actions . . .
I am so. Anyway. (*He sings again and does the actions.*)

If I Live To Be One Hundred.
I Will Never Know From Where
(Nose From Whey-Hair.) . . .
Came Those Lovely. Scarlet Ribbons.

Scarlet Ribbons. For Her Hair.
('Four' Her Hair.)

What did yeh think of that? Huh? Deadly? That's good.
Go to sleep now like a good girl and I'll see you tomorrow.
Yeah, in the afternoon. What do yeh think we're goin' to
do? What do we do every Steven's Day? Yeah well that's
what we'll do tomorrow too. Go to sleep now and put Derek
back on to me. Alright. Night hon . . .

MAEVE *moves around the shop in a state of distress,
gazing into the living quarters etc.*

Derek! What are yeh up to? Over . . . Yeah . . . No I'm not
in the yard now, I'm on the roof. Over. No, the flat roof.
Piled up with snow. I'm knee deep in it here man. Yeah, I can
see half the town from here. Little Tommy Day goin' by and
everything. I just hit him in the back of the neck with a
snowball. He's wonderin' where it came from. He sees me.
He's singin'. Can yeh hear him? No. Hang on. (*He holds the
walkie-talkie away from him and sings in a crooner voice.*)

When The Evening Shadows Fall.
And You're Wondering Who To Call.
Look Around And You Will See.
There's Always Me.

Can yeh hear him? It's not me. Hang on . . .

If Your Great Romance Should End.
And You're Lonesome For A Friend.
For A Little Company . . .

There's a bit of a crowd gatherin' round him now. They're
peltin' him with snowballs . . . One went right into his
mouth. He's still singin' though, fair play to him. There's
Always Me. Alright then, go on. The biggest drawback in
the jungle? Yeah I know yeh told me. And the constipated
mathematician, I know. Put them away now will yeh and
don't let your mother see any more of them. (*To* MAEVE.)
Eddie got me these Christmas crackers. They're filthy. It's
a good job Pauline's mother didn't go up to her for dinner
that's all I can say. Derek I've to go . . . I have to . . . You're
breakin' up on me. (*He makes a crackling sound.*) . . . No,

can't make yeh out at all . . . Over and out . . . see yeh
tomorrow . . . (*He puts the walkie-talkie away.*) . . . He's a
handful. Never stops.

MAEVE (*sitting beside him now*). I'm sorry Oweney.

OWENEY (*takes her hand*). What can yeh do? . . . My portrait
survived anyway. Yeh shouldn't have. . . . I'm still wantin'
my scarf back mind yeh . . . How did yeh get on today?

MAEVE. Ah, yeh know . . . What did you do?

OWENEY. Meself and Leonard went down as far as the Whole
Hog for our dinner. Little Tommy Day was down there with
all the other lonely hearts. It was alright though. It was nice.
I went up to the house for my tea – to see the kids and that.
Sharon was out for a walk with her boyfriend so it all
worked out alright. She came back right at the wrong time
though. Pauline broke down in the hall as I was leavin'.
Sharon thought I'd upset her or somethin' and she reared
up on me. It ended up with the three of us cryin' in the hall
with our arms around each other. Your man's gone back to
his missus apparently. I didn't even know he had one . . .
I came back then to this . . . I suppose you got it between
the eyes too did yeh?

MAEVE. Yeh might say that. . . . He took the shop back. He
said it was costing him money – a thousand a week or
somethin'.

OWENEY. How did he make that out?

MAEVE. Oh I don't know. He had it all written down like –
on paper. Yeh know it all made sense on paper. I mean
I couldn't really argue with that. Yeh know the facts and
figures like . . . He wants to move to Kildare now he says.
He's after buyin' a sort of a stud farm or somethin'. He's all
into horses all of a sudden. The thing is I don't want to go to
Kildare 'cause I don't know anyone there. I mean I hardly
knew anyone here until I met you. I feel like a geisha or
somethin' to tell yeh the truth – goin' where I'm put.

OWENEY. Don't go to Kildare. Stay here with me. I'll sell P.J.
this place and we'll set up in the Mall together. I'm serious.
I'm dyin' about you and you know I am! . . . Don't go. Stay.

MAEVE (*puts her head on his shoulder*). I wish I could
    Oweney but I can't.

OWENEY. Why not? . . . Huh? . . . Why not?

MAEVE. Oh I don't know . . . I mean he is my husband
    Oweney yeh know. And he's the loneliest creature I've ever
    seen. I mean you think I'm bad, He's ten times worse. No
    one ever calls for him Oweney yeh know – to go for a pint
    or somethin'. Yeh know? Like ever like! I mean he goes
    around actin' all superior and all but he must be wonderin'
    why no one ever calls for him. I mean yeh would, wouldn't
    yeh? I just wish someone had the nerve to take him down a
    peg or two for me sometime 'cause he's too high and mighty
    for his own good if you ask me . . . Maybe if he had a
    family or somethin'.

OWENEY. Where's he now?

MAEVE. He's outside there. Paradin'.

OWENEY. One of these days boy.

MAEVE. Forget it Oweney. (OWENEY *scoffs.*) What? You
    think this is the worst he can do or somethin'? This is not
    the worst he can do yeh know.

OWENEY. I'm not afraid of him.

MAEVE. He could burn the place down while you're asleep in
    your bed some night.

OWENEY. My family's been here for generations Maeve.

MAEVE. Or shoot yeh. Murder yeh. Dump your body in the
    river or somewhere.

OWENEY. Like generations like yeh know. I mean if you
    think now that some little jumped up whatdoyoucallit is
    goin' to . . .

MAEVE. Listen to me Oweney will yeh. Listen to me . . .

OWENEY. I mean who made him lord of the dance anyway.
    'Cause all this stuff he does yeh know . . .

MAEVE. Shh Oweney . . . Oweney shh . . .

OWENEY. . . . means nothin' to me. Like nothin' like yeh know. And I'll say it straight to his face too.

MAEVE. Stop now. (*She hushes him up and indicates that P.J. is nearby.*)

OWENEY. I'm not worried about him Maeve.

MAEVE. I know . . . I know . . . Shh.

OWENEY. See you're forgettin' that I went to school with him Maeve and I don't mind tellin' yeh he was no great shakes then and he's even less shakes now – in my book anyway.

MAEVE. Yeah well forget about all that now. I want yeh to forget about that and I want yeh to do somethin' for me. I need yeh to do somethin'.

OWENEY. Yeah? What?

MAEVE. I want yeh to try to live to be old Oweney.

OWENEY. Yeh what?

MAEVE. I want yeh to live to be old and I want you to promise me that when I'm gone you'll never forget me.

OWENEY. That's two things and I couldn't forget you even if I wanted to.

MAEVE. Good. That's good. And then you can tell all the other old fellas who come in and out of here in twenty or thirty years time or whenever all about me yeh see. And when yeh do I want you to exaggerate Oweney. I want you to blow me out of all proportion. Your love for me and mine for you. 'Cause I want to go down in history Oweney, yeh know – somebody's history, anybody's history. And then I'll live forever yeh see. And so will you. The two of us will live forever. 'He told her to look in the river,' they'll say, 'and what she saw was lovely. What she saw . . . was beautiful.'

Pause as they turn to look into the fallen, cracked mirror. The image resembles one of MATT's *paintings. Pause.*

I wouldn't be good for you anyway Oweney. Better off without me really – when all's said and done like. Ask anyone . . . Ask P.J . . . Anyway you have to try and get back to your own house Oweney . . . 'Cause I hate to think of you livin' here all on your own yeh know. Promise me you will. Try at least. I know it's hard but you have to try and get back. And I have to try too – to make it work. I have to try and make somethin' work Oweney 'cause at the end of the day it's a reflection on me if I don't. Yeh know? (*She takes his scarf from around her neck and hangs it on* OWENEY.) . . . Besides all that, your heart is already spoken for if you ask me. I mean it's not really mine to take or yours to give away.

She kisses him – a long, slow, lingering farewell.
LEONARD *appears in the doorway. Pause.* MAEVE *leaves.*

LEONARD. What happened here Oweney?

OWENEY (*miles away*). Huh?

LEONARD. They didn't wreck upstairs as well Oweney did they? 'Cause Sally's thinkin' of movin' out of St Mary's tomorrow or the next day and movin' in here with me if that's alright with you Oweney . . . Matt. (*He hurries to* MATT *on the landing.*) Oweney . . . Oweney . . .

OWENEY. What? (*He goes to them.*) What's wrong with him? What happened?

MATT. Two fellas jumped me in the alley.

OWENEY. Who was it?

MATT. I don't know. Two Dublin fellas. I managed to get away from them and they followed me over here. They kicked in the door of the shop then and I could hear them wreckin' the place below. I looked down to see your man P.J. standing in the hall sort of whatdoyoucallit . . . I don't know . . . supervisin' it or somethin'. He told me to tell yeh in case you're wonderin' Oweney that it was The Jack Of Hearts. Tell him it was the Jack Of Hearts, he said. . . . I'm sorry Oweney.

OWENEY. You're alright. Don't worry about it . . . Take him inside Leonard.

LEONARD. Yeah, right . . . What are you goin' to do Oweney?

OWENEY *goes down to the shop.*

OWENEY. P.J . . . Two hundred smackers!

OWENEY *takes some money from the cashbox, takes the painting of himself from the wall and exits to the street. LEONARD helps MATT into his bedsit where he finds EDDIE asleep in the chair.*

LEONARD. Eddie!

EDDIE. Huh?

LEONARD. What are you doin' here?

EDDIE. Well that's nice alright. I pop in to see me auld mate to wish him a happy Christmas and all the rest of it and he treats me like an intruder or somethin'.

LEONARD. I've no money for yeh Eddie. I mean between the court case and havin' to buy Sally a Christmas present and all . . .

EDDIE. Whooo, slow down will yeh . . . I'm not here lookin' for money! I mean it's Christmas night for fuck's sake. And me aunty Cissy is over in the mortuary. I mean what kind of a man do you think I am, eh? Hah? I mean . . . I'm here to give not to take.

LEONARD. Yeah?

EDDIE. Yeah. I mean . . . What happened him?

LEONARD. Two fellas jumped him in the alley . . . P.J.

EDDIE *thinks about it and shrugs as* LEONARD *puts MATT lying on the bed and proceeds to nurse his wounds with a damp cloth etc.*

EDDIE. I stepped over him on the stairs earlier on there alright. I thought he just had a few jars in him.

LEONARD. They're after wreckin' the place below too.

EDDIE. So I see . . . Anyway here's twenty towards your expenses and that and for keepin' your mouth shut and all the rest of it. I appreciate it yeh know. Alright?

LEONARD. Yeah. Great. Thanks Eddie. Sorry about your Aunt Cissy.

EDDIE. Yeah well so am I yeh know. 'Cause she was a nice woman yeh know. A very nice woman. Sure me uncle Riche'd put years on yeh anyway. Hey you don't say nothin' to Oweney about me givin' you that twenty, do yeh hear me?

LEONARD (*at the window*). Yeah, right.

EDDIE. I'll tell him meself after . . . Jaysus they gave him a right hidin'. Ah well . . . I told them . . . I warned them all . . . What's goin' on out there now?

LEONARD. Oweney and P.J. are boxin' in the snow.

EDDIE. Yeah? . . . Who's winnin'?

LEONARD. It looks fairly even at the moment although Oweney is startin' to get the better of him now I think. Oh! . . . Nice punch Oweney.

EDDIE. Is P.J. down?

LEONARD. He is now.

EDDIE. Anyone bleedin'?

LEONARD. I don't know. I'd say so. There's money all over the place.

EDDIE. Lovely. There's nothin' like a bit of blood in the snow boy! I hit big Craig Carty outside a disco one snowy night – wham – he went down like a bag of shit.

LEONARD. Oweney is gone into the little boutique. Your man's missus is standin' over him.

EDDIE. I mean it was fairly nasty lookin' yeh know. But the blood in the snow was beautiful to behold. Although I'd say this looks nicer than that because your man didn't have no woman to cradle him nor nothin' yeh know.

LEONARD. She's not cradlin' him. She's just standin' over him that's all – helpin' him up and that.

EDDIE. Mind you Craigy was an ugly bastard at the best of times – by anyone's standards.

LEONARD. Huh? . . . Here's Oweney now . . . (*He calls out and struggles to open the window.*) Oweney . . . Oweney . . . Oweney . . . He don't hear me . . . What do yeh think'll happen to Oweney after this Eddie?

EDDIE. Nothin'. Big Hank Thomas is in Mountjoy and I'm on me night off and the two goons are gone back to Dublin so . . . She won't let nothin' happen him anyway. He's protected as they say – from on high! . . . Oweney though, hah? One in a million boy! (*He sings.*)

May The Lord Have Mercy On Such As We.
Ba Ba Ba . . . (*He bleats.*)

EDDIE *laughs. So does* LEONARD, *nervously. Lights down on the bedsit. Lights rise on the shop.* OWENEY *enters with the painting of* MAEVE. RICHIE *is at his heels.*

OWENEY. If I want to admire meself Richie I'll look in the mirror. Anyway it's high time someone took that fella down a peg or two if yeh ask me. And another thing I told him out straight that he's not gettin' this place either. Not now, not ever. 'Cause it's not for sale I mean this shop was here long before me and it'll be here long after me too if I can help it. I mean what's he goin' to put in its place anyway? Hah? Neon? Plastic? Hollow crap? Well I'm here to tell yeh that there's nothin' hollow about this place mate. And there's nothin' hollow about me either. I mean to say I have skills yeh know – number ones, number twos, number threes, skinheads, mohicans, whatever yeh like – hot towels, neck shaves, close shaves, regular shaves, the works. I mean . . . Oweney's fuckin' Rendezvous mate!

RICHIE. Sure I know.

OWENEY. And I delivered my message loud and clear too Richie I don't mind tellin' yeh – from Oweney Clark Junior boy says I to him – the third!

RICHIE. The third?

OWENEY (*he shrugs*). . . . What are they doin' out there now?

RICHIE. What? (*He goes to the window.*)

LEONARD (*to* EDDIE *above*). She's helpin' him into the car Eddie.

EDDIE. Is he badly hurt?

RICHIE. He's limpin' a bit that's all. Looks like a newborn baby – all covered in snow.

OWENEY. Is she lookin' over here?

LEONARD. Yeah. A little wave from her. She's goin' around to the driver's side now. She's givin' your man the picture of Oweney to hold. She looks queer nice from here boy!

OWENEY. She's a faraway woman though Richie yeh know. A faraway woman boy!

LEONARD. Well she's fairly far away now anyway Eddie because she's gone.

OWENEY. Huh?

RICHIE. She's gone Oweney.

Sad pause.

RICHIE. What are yeh goin' to do now Oweney?

OWENEY. I don't know Richie – die a little or somethin' I suppose.

RICHIE. Huh?

OWENEY *looks at the painting.*

OWENEY. Yeh can just see her though Richie can't yeh? – ridin' like a tiger cross the plains of Kildare!

RICHIE. Yeh what?

OWENEY *nurses his swollen hand and looks around at the devastation.*

OWENEY. I may go up home to me own house Richie I think. Maybe Pauline won't let me in of course but sure I'll give her a knock anyway. She might let me sleep on the couch or somethin', hah? (*He stuffs the walkie-talkie into his pocket and empties the cash box.*) I mean it's Christmas night like . . . Yeh know?

OWENEY *puts on his coat and scarf etc. puts all the lights out and they exit to the hall. He tries in vain to shut the buckled door of the shop. He glances at the mess and shrugs it off.* EDDIE *is coming down the stairs as* LEONARD *heads* MATT *back to his own room.*

OWENEY. What were you doin' up there?

EDDIE. I called in to wish me auld mate a Happy Christmas, why?

OWENEY. Just wonderin'.

EDDIE (*surveying the mess*). Jaysus, hah! . . . What's all this I hear about you doin' the locomotion in the snow boy?

OWENEY. What's it to you if I was?

EDDIE. Hah? (*He cowers away from* OWENEY *in mock fear.*)

OWENEY. Yeh big galoot yeh!

EDDIE. Hah? . . .

He grabs OWENEY *around the neck and wrestles his head in under his armpit playfully.*

OWENEY. Come up off of me will yeh, yeh big feckin' ejit yeh . . . Come on, till I lock the place up . . .

EDDIE. Give me that snowball there Richie . . .

OWENEY. Come out of it I said, yeh big fat lump of . . .

EDDIE. What?

He bends to scoop up a snowball which he rams into OWENEY*'s face and down the back of his neck etc. as* LEONARD *crosses the landing to his own room*

OWENEY. Yeh dirty, rotten, stinkin', son of a bitch yeh . . .

EDDIE. Hah? Huh? (*They are out on the street now.*)

RICHIE. Will I bang this door or what Oweney?

OWENEY. Yeh big, fat, lump of . . . shit on a swingswong . . . Ah!

EDDIE. A big, fat lump of what? Hah? A big fat lump of what did you say?

EDDIE lets him go and runs away. OWENEY, *in a fury, chases him off with a snowball.*

OWENEY. Yeh big, fat, lump of . . .

RICHIE bangs the door and looks up at the sky.

RICHIE (*to himself*). It's goin' to snow again too I'd say.

He exits.

Lights rise on the bedsit. LEONARD *is in his pyjamas, cleaning his teeth. He crosses the room, blesses himself and gets into bed. He lies down and turns over, away from us. Through the window we can see the snow softly falling.*

Lights down.

I Once Loved a Sailor Boy

Words (on pages 40-41) and music by Billy Roche

Acknowledgements

The publishers are grateful for permission to reproduce lyrics from the following songs:

p. 23 The Last Waltz, words and music by Les Reed and Barry Mason, © 1967. Reproduced by permission of Donna Music Ltd, London WC2H 0QY

p. 23 Living Doll, words and music by Lionel Bart, © 1959. Reproduced by permission of Peter Maurice Music Co Ltd, London WC2H 0QY

p. 24 Holy Cow, words and music by Allen Toussaint, ©1966. Reproduced by permission of Ardmore & Beechwood Ltd, London WC2H 0QY

p. 27 Love is a Many Splendoured Thing, words by Paul Francis Webster, music by Sammy Fain, © 1955 (renewed) EMI Catalog Partnership, EMI Miller Catalog Inc and EMI United Partnership Ltd, USA. Worldwide print rights controlled by Warner Bros Publications Inc/ IMP Ltd. Reproduced by permission of International Music Publications Ltd. All rights reserved.

p. 31 Boys, words and music by Wes Farrell and Luther Dixon, © 1961, Ludix Music Inc USA. Reproduced by permission of EMI Music Publishing Ltd, London WC2H 0QY.

p. 31-32 The Answer to Everything, words by Bob Hilliard, © 1961 by Better Half Music Co. Copyright renewed. All rights reserved. International copyright secured, Printed with permission from Bourne Music Ltd.

p. 35 Santa Claus is Comin' To Town, words by Haven Gillespie, music by Fred Coots, © 1934 EMI Catalogue Partnership, EMI Feist Catalog Inc and EMI United Partnership Ltd, USA. Worldwide print rights controlled by Warner Bros Publications Inc/IMP Ltd. Reproduced by permission of International Music Publications Ltd. All rights reserved.

A Nick Hern Book

On Such As We first published in Great Britain and the
Republic of Ireland in 2001 as a paperback original by
Nick Hern Books, 14 Larden Road, London W3 7ST

On Such As We copyright © 2001 by Billy Roche

Typeset by Country Setting, Kingsdown, Kent CT14 8ES
Printed by Biddles, Guildford

A CIP catalogue record for this book is available from the
British Library

ISBN 1 85459 671 3